The

Nature

of

Bliss

The

Nature

of

Bliss

Balance Love Integrity Sexuality Soul

MAUREEN MOSS

Sidney House Publishing

Published by
Sidney House Publishing
2305-C Ashland St., Suite 405
Ashland, Oregon   97520

Publisher's Cataloging-in-Publication
(Provided by Quality Books, Inc.)

Moss, Maureen
    The nature of bliss : balance, love, integrity,
sexuality, soul / Maureen Moss.
    p. cm.
    LCCN 2002090487
    ISBN 0-9717971-2-9

    1. Self-realization. 2. Love. 3. Metaphysics.
    I. Title.

BF637.S4M67 2002   158.1
                      QBI02-701284

Cover and interior design: Mayapriya Long, www.bookwrights.com
Cover photo: Brad Wrobleski / Masterfile

Printed in Canada

This book is dedicated to all who are striving for clarity

Contents

Acknowledgments   ix

Preface   xi

Introduction:
Life Is What We Think It Is   1

1. *B* alance   13

2. *L* ove   43

3. *I* ntegrity   77

4. *S* exuality   111

5. *S* oul   159

About the Author   209

Acknowledgments

To acknowledge those who have assisted me in numerous ways to bring this book to life is as important to me as every page that I have written.

First I want to thank God, the Source of love and creativity that fueled this book. In harmony with God, I wish to thank every angel, guide, and teacher of the Light that assisted in bringing the information from above to below—from my heart to the printed page.

I would also like to extend deep gratitude and love to the following:

To my spiritual sister and teacher Linda Filipiak, who more than once helped me gather the parts of myself that I had left in various places over the years and bring them back home.

To my precious spiritual sister Renee Morgan Brooks, a gift from God who came along when I was certain that God had gone on vacation—forever. Thank you, Renee, for showing me what love looks like, so I had a go-by for the first time in my life.

To Kate and Al DeWayne, who hold many positions in my life: adopted parents, dear friends, sounding boards, support group, short-order editors, spiritual advisors, and great eating buddies!

To Neal Potts, who held the vision of this book and my abilities long before I did.

To Kate "Schtee" Hansen, for twenty years of always being there for me, always loving, and always, without exception, knowing how to be an unconditional friend.

To Candace and Eddie Van Hout, who are shining examples of love in action as partners together, and as sacred friends in my life.

To Frank Dulcich, for opening your heart to me at the perfect time.

To Margaret "Pebby" Kuan, for putting love into action.

To Sammy Spayd, an angel who flew in from "somewhere out there" to enrich my life as I came to the finish line. Thank you for alleviating pressure, making me laugh, sending me a Christmas tree (decorated, no less), and buying presents for my kitty cat.

To Stephanie Marohn, my editor who didn't make my life a living hell! Thank you for your integrity, your presence, and your excellence.

And finally, I give deep thanks for my angel in fur, Sidney. I acknowledge that I am truly blessed.

Preface

Each of us has a gap between our authentic nature and our everyday life.

We compromise ourselves by holding on to the illusion that we are not enough—that we are not talented enough, beautiful enough, lovable enough, intelligent enough, important enough, or wealthy enough. This is nothing new for the mind of humankind. Our stories are steeped in mental minutiae that rule our lives, with the result that very little new is actually possible. It is clear that the old way is not working, as we watch systems, institutions, communities, countries, and individuals break down everywhere.

You may have noticed by now that you are no longer able to rely on familiar myths and survival methods of trickery that focus on the small I am of Who You Are. The Universe has issued a wake-up call, again and perhaps finally, and is asking in earnest that we shed the deception of our controlled separate lives and begin in earnest the journey back to our true nature: balance, love, integrity, sexuality, and soul in harmony. This is the nature of bliss.

It is time to stand on Holy Ground in the midst of your personal transformation. It is time to strive for a clear mental sky, where your true nature shines radiantly, separation dissolves, and all merge into One. It is time to give birth to the best that is within you.

Are you aware that you are a Source of immense power and of exceptional value, not only in the restoration of this planet, but also in the healing of the heart of every person alive? You have the power to alter the human condition because there is but one human condition, and each of us reflects, influences, and *is* that condition. What condition are you in? What are you adding to or subtracting from humanity?

If you consider the magnitude of this reality, then making tracks now to liberate yourself from your old way of life will become top priority. The path back from self-abandonment, the bleeding of your heart, and the sadness in your psyche is to return to your true nature. There is nothing more important for the planet and the future of humankind than for every person to become free. If you are compelled, or intuitively attracted to freedom, then come within the pages you hold in your hands.

Once inside *The Nature of Bliss,* you will lose the desire to find refuge in that which is false. Instead, you will discover the almost unbearable ecstasy that occurs when one returns to one's Self, one's true nature. You will find the human condition healing as you take your authentic, unique, necessary, balanced self out into the world and live your life's purpose. You will come to understand why you are here and you will live your life to prove it possible. Once returned to your true nature, you will be dazzled by your love affair with humanity and your mind will have no fixed notion about Who You Are.

INTRODUCTION

Life Is What We Think It Is

I have spent a good part of my life looking for peace of mind, and another good part looking for the perfect relationship. I believed that peace of mind went hand in glove with the perfect relationship. I searched for that relationship in nightclubs and restaurants, at seminars and retreats. My friends tried to help me find him via their friends and friends of friends. I searched in California and Boston, from Tahoe to Texas. Where was he? I knew he was out there somewhere, just waiting to meet me. Year after year, I depleted the soil of the earth with my footsteps circling outside myself to find my "other half." I thought that if I found that just-right relationship, I would find peace of mind at long last. I was right and I was wrong.

When someone would ask me what I would wish for if I had one wish, I would always respond, "Peace of mind." I never wished for a new house or to win the lottery. I never wished for a fancy Jaguar or a vacation home in the islands. I wished for peace of mind, just peace of mind. Simply saying the words 'peace of mind' made me breathe more freely.

Even as a child, somewhere deep within me, I seemed to know that if I had peace of mind, everything else would follow. What I didn't know was where to find it. Growing up, I was told that if I went to college, found a good man, settled down, and had a family, I'd be happy. You couldn't find evidence of that by looking at my family but, because that's what I was told, that's what I believed—sort of.

I was a product of my environment. I had no reason not to accept what I was taught, shown, or told. We learn by example. Somewhere inside me, however, there was a tiny voice saying the "teachers" I had didn't get it—whatever "it" was. But while I was growing up, the little voice was very faint and the words around me very loud.

I was a confused child who always felt like a stranger in a strange land. Things appeared hazy to me, not bright or clear. It seemed that I should have come with an instruction manual, if not for me, then at least for my parents. I never felt that I was raised in a family. There were two people called mom and dad; soon came another person called stepmother, along with two half-brothers, who had another person called dad, and later a person called a half-sister arrived. Everyone fought and yelled. All but two lived under one roof. I witnessed them raise the roof, raise their voices, and raise hell, but it didn't seem like they were raising me. I didn't think I was very important, considering everything else that was going on, so I just tried to raise myself.

The word *raise* means to lift up. Imagine what would happen if parents knew that their assignment was to lift up their children! As the Bible tells us, when God raises us, "we are lifted to greater heights."

In the attempt to raise myself, in whatever direction I turned, whether inside or outside myself, there were brambles and thickets and winding roads that always seemed to come back to the same place: confusion, fear, and unrest. I felt that my very thoughts were toxic. My stepmother told me numerous times that I would never amount to anything and that no one would ever want me. Although I swore I would prove her wrong, deep down I believed her.

Coming from a fragmented family, which wasn't prepared to bring love to me, to themselves, or to each other, I never saw what love really looks like. Love was an unmapped path in our house and anger was the road well traveled. When I got hit, yelled at, or humiliated, the people who called themselves my parents told me that it was because they loved me, it was for my own good. I didn't like or understand this version of love, so it seemed like a good idea to create my own and go find it somewhere else. I had a big job in front of me: find peace of mind, the perfect relationship, and love. Which way to Oz?

Arriving into adulthood from these painful beginnings, I fed myself from the trough of despair and hopelessness. My mind was out of control and so I turned to my ego, which was more than willing to step in and "help." The ego seemed to give me some kind of power, some sort of elevated status, and I noticed that those around me were buying into the act. I didn't know then that the ego was the defender of my fears and false beliefs about who I was. I believed I wasn't good enough and my ego said, "So what if you're not good enough! Fake it—no one will ever know the difference." So I mastered the art of deception. No one

3

was more deceived than I. For years, I had no idea where the real me ended and the lies began.

My mind tricked me into believing that I was a victim of my childhood. I trusted that belief when it pointed out the inadequacies of everyone around me and the terribly unloving experiences that first my family and later my boyfriends, lovers, and husbands bestowed upon me. My ego said, "You're tough as nails, you've got everything under control, keep pushing ahead." But I continued to wonder who I was.

Then there came a time when I quit wondering and just accepted the confusion and turmoil. "Life is a bitch, get used to it," I told myself. I became quite adept at surviving, never realizing that on the other side of surviving lay thriving. What kept me in the swim of survival was my constant struggle against the currents of life—and my belief that there was no God, there was just me. I wept from a place that shed no visible tears.

I went from job to job, then started up and closed down companies. I called myself an entrepreneur, had a couple of husbands and a bunch of affairs. By the time I was thirty-eight, I felt sixty-eight. I was literally sick and tired of being sick and tired. Physically, emotionally, mentally, and spiritually, I was spent. I had given myself the dis-eases of Epstein-Barr virus and chronic fatigue syndrome. I had looked everywhere and to everyone for peace. I had turned inward again and again, wondering if the answers lay there.

Back then, turning inward meant going inside my head to try to figure things out. I kept analyzing my life in my mind. I was asking my mind, which had created the problems, to solve the problems. My thoughts kept telling me that there was nothing wrong with me that a good, loving relationship couldn't heal. I didn't realize that a relationship involved the heart and soul, not thoughts and the ego. My mind was the strongest, most used muscle in my body, my heart the weakest. Later, I came to learn that what I thought was my heart speaking was really my mind trying to convince me that my thoughts were heartfelt.

One Saturday evening, I was at a friend's home for a dinner party. I was having one conversation while listening to another and caught the words, "The definition of insanity is doing the same thing over and over again and thinking that something is going to change." I was certain I'd heard those words before, but this evening they carried new meaning. This was the synopsis of my life: doing the same things over and over again, behaving the same way, continuously analyzing and judging myself and everyone else, and repeatedly having the same expectations from different people—and thinking that something was going to change. At that moment, something new and unfamiliar stirred inside me, as if someone I couldn't see had come to help me—finally.

I left the party, went home, and sat in my darkened living room with one candle burning. I pleaded to a God I didn't know to help me, and then I got still.

Something moved inside my being. Energy that I had never felt before moved through me. I sat perfectly still so as not to disturb whatever it was. The tiny voice that had been deep inside me since I was a child moved up to the area of my heart. I *felt*, not thought, that my life was about to change dramatically. I didn't know how, but I instinctively knew I didn't need to know. For once I didn't have to figure anything out. I would be guided. I heard the little voice tell me that I was to go silently within, not inside my head, but deep inside my heart, and feel, not think. This, I heard, was where my life's instruction manual was kept.

I had never done this before. I was to go past my mind, deep inside to the silence between my thoughts to meet the peace of mind, the love, and the relationship that I had so craved from everyone else. I was to go inside my heart to hear the voice of an unseen energy and find the buried treasure—my own love. Everything I had ever wanted, desired, wished, pleaded, and prayed for had always been there. It was my job to excavate it. I was reminded of Glinda, the good witch in *The Wizard of Oz*, when she said to Dorothy, "You've always had it, my dear, you've always had it."

The sounds of silence were the most magnificent sounds I had ever heard and I stayed silent for sixty-two hours—just over two and a half days. The first glimmers of my true nature started to emerge and my experience of bliss was being born. My life began.

The journey to the center of myself—my heart, my soul, my authentic nature—was the journey of a mystic. I had no idea how to get to where I was going, and I had a feeling that it wouldn't be easy. So I asked God (in whom I still didn't fully believe, but who else to ask?) to send help. And God did. It is true that when the student is ready, the teacher(s) appears. I was sent angels in the flesh: an amazing spiritual healer with eyes so big and blue it seemed I was looking into the eyes of the sky; and another whose mere presence made me know for the first time what love really looks like. They both seemed to appear "out of the blue" within two weeks of each other. I called them my "angel bookends." Although I wasn't aware of it at the time, I was also sent angels and guides from above. Little did I know then how loved I was, how loved we all are by the Universe. The angels and guides were only waiting for me to surrender my thoughts and my control so there would be room for them to come in and help me.

This was a new challenge. I was accustomed to being in complete control, thinking I had to be or nothing would work the way I thought it should. I had always set my own course—haphazard as it may have appeared to some—and steered my own ship. I had navigated my ship in the way I knew best since, after all, survival in rough waters was my specialty.

I will not tell you that this new journey was easy, or that things changed overnight. I experienced old behavior patterns dying off—some slowly and painfully—but then a clearer, brighter, grander version of myself was awakened. There were moments in my journey when it felt like I was riding on a train with the windows blacked out—I couldn't see where I was going, yet it seemed I was going forward. That was the point—not to be sure. I had to learn to trust in a process that wasn't defined by a game plan and offered no predictions of outcome in the way we humans have come to expect. I had to give up seeing what I was used to seeing, in order to see more clearly from a different perspective.

Everything that was familiar to me dissolved. My business went through a death and reemerged, my friendships changed, my likes and dislikes changed—*I* changed. I looked around to see where I was, and I wasn't sure. I was somewhere between here and there. When I asked questions, I didn't receive answers in the way I was accustomed—the answers came through my heart, not my ears. They came not from the mind of Maureen but from a higher source, which I call God.

This new journey required fresh and untried equipment, tools I'd never used—faith, courage, trust, compassion toward others and myself, and surrender. I had no way of knowing how long it would take, but I knew I would need to exercise daily vigilance and diligence, and be willing to accept help from others. I would have to learn the difference between the wisdom of the heart, the calling of the soul, and the directives of the logical mind and, with increased understanding, bring them into balance. That was the key: bringing everything I knew myself to be—the flawed *and* the flawless—into balance. It was time to accept all of me, to receive the blessing of self-acceptance. It was the beginning of a life I couldn't have envisioned for myself because, through thought alone, we cannot even begin to imagine what the Universe can create through us and for us.

I would never have believed that my mind could become so still that I could hear the soft voices of angels. My life has become a moving meditation because of my commitment to myself, which means attending to the voice that speaks to me through the center of my heart and leads me into fulfilling my Divine purpose here on Earth. The commitment has uncompromising priorities—that no time, place, person, or thing takes precedence over the remembering of who I Am: a child of God, a spiritual being having a human experience, a light on this earth meant to touch and be touched by love.

I have come to realize that life is about the coexistence of opposites. We must have pain in order to know joy, we must know suspicion in order to understand trust, and we must experience the loss of our true nature in order to rejoice when we come back to it. We must experience the scattering of our thoughts and emotions so that we can marvel at ourselves when we realize we have the ability to bring ourselves back into harmonious balance by our breath alone.

I was right when I thought that if only I could find that perfect relationship, I would find inner peace. I was wrong when I thought it would come from another person. I had to create that relationship with the Divine and, once that was established, everything that was natural began to pour forth.

I wrote this book to provide what I hope will be more than a source of information. Yes, I provide keys and strategies for taking the journey to bliss, but it is you who will use them to gain insight and step onto the path that will lead you back to your true nature—the nature of bliss. In order for you to reach a higher level in your life, it is important to act, rather than react. Then you will wake up to the truth of Who You Really Are—a spiritual being no longer diminished by the human lies you have been told by yourself and others. We have spent lifetime upon lifetime with very little progress of the soul. Our preoccupations have precluded our enlightenment. Most people leave the planet with such a small amount of soul growth that when they reemerge in human form, they experience the same pitfalls again, only played out in a different scenario. Whether in a past lifetime you were a king or a pauper, a prostitute or a princess, makes no difference. It is karma (the seeds of memory that reside in the soul that we carry with us from one incarnation to the next) and what we do with it, how we recreate it, that makes all the difference to our experience now and later.

If you think the journey to your authentic nature is going to be tough, know that only your thoughts about the journey will make it more or less difficult. There were times that my thoughts made it tougher for me than it had to be. There were also days when the grace of God and the changes that I witnessed in myself brought me to my knees in tears of joy and great relief, providing me with a glimpse of my dream—inner peace. The journey was what it was. Your mind can no more know what lies ahead of you than your car can fly you to Florida.

Nobody takes the journey to bliss alone. Our traveling partners—our angels and guides in the seen and the unseen—bless us; they take every step of the journey with us. But first we must ask for their help and mean it. It is our persevering and attention along the way that attract more angels, guides, and teachers in the seen and the unseen than you can ever imagine. They know when we reach the pivotal points—where the earth seems to drop out from under us—and it is by angel wings and the love of God that we are lifted up and set down right where we need to be.

When I began the deep healing and "re-membering" of myself (the process of putting the parts of me back together into one balanced whole), one of my wonderful spiritual healers said to me, "Maureen, you are an extremely smart woman. You can quote almost every author of the hundreds of books you have read about life, how it works, and what makes it not work. You give brilliant seminars. Yet you still go home to the same struggles you had before. You have spent well over thirty years intellectualizing the answers to life. You talk the talk eloquently, but you have integrated very little. Now it's time to bring the walk and the talk together." In other words, little had changed except the expansion of my knowledge. She reminded me that wisdom is knowledge applied.

Someone once sent a card to me with the message: "When you come to the edge of all of the light that you know, one of two things will happen: you will be given something solid to stand on or you will be taught to fly." My personal journey has led me to know this and know it in every corner of my heart. You have my promise that it is true. I can give you this promise because there really is no separation between you and me. We have all experienced the same issues, at one time or another, and from one extreme to another— only the details of our stories are different.

Lack of self-worth has many faces and shows up in our work, in our relationships, and in our minds. Addictions also manifest in different ways, yet all are a form of suppression of our true feelings. Our judgments of ourselves and others may be pervasive or subtle, but they are still judgments. Whether we abandon others or ourselves, it is still abandonment. Whether internalized or exhibited for all to see, anger and rage exist. When we don't trust ourselves, we don't trust the process of Life. Life includes all of us, with experiences of things both perfect and imperfect.

I was guided to write this book to help you live your true life without becoming lost in your experiences.

The acronym BLISS—Balance, Love, Integrity, Sexuality, and Soul—was sent to me in a meditation. My life had already taught me that when these five elements are in harmony, the result is bliss.

The Nature of Bliss is meant to invite you into yourself. I pray that you will be moved in the deepest part of your soul to remember your true nature and experience bliss—to move from the perspective of fear and doubt to the perspective of love and courage. And by the grace of God, this book will help you.

Thus we begin the journey.

CHAPTER 1

*B*alance

Except ye be converted and become as little children
ye shall not enter into the Kingdom of Heaven.
—Jesus of Nazareth, Matt. 18:3

Once upon a time we had the distinct pleasure of being children. We could still see the wings of the angels although we were far from home. We had vivid imaginations that allowed us to have close friendships with imaginary friends. We had not yet made up our minds as to who we were. Our underdeveloped egos allowed us to experience the wonder of the Universe, which inspired rather than defined us. Vulnerability came naturally because it was an integral part of us. We giggled with glee when someone made funny faces or a puppy knocked us to the ground to bathe us with loving licks. Nature fascinated us. We would quiet down to witness the progression of a ladybug crawling on our hand and tickling us as each little leg made its way up our arm. We sang to the stars, "Twinkle, twinkle, little star, how I wonder what you are." And before we went to bed, we got down on our little knees and prayed to God our souls to keep. As children, we took for granted that this natural way of life was the way life was.

When we went to the park to play, we chose our playmates based on who was near, not on a litany of judgment about each person. We didn't care if they were chubby, skinny, had crooked teeth or brand new clothes. And we chose what to do—swing, slide, or seesaw—depending on how we felt at that moment.

Do you remember when you were a child playing on the seesaw with a new friend? The sun was shining, the birds were singing, and you could hear the excited squeals and shrieks of other children at play in the park. Some were on the jungle gym, some were swinging on the swings, others were zooming down a winding slide. They didn't distract you—you weren't competing with them, or sizing them up, or registering a first impression. They were just children being children, playing and having fun just like you.

Remember when you and your friend would laugh with delight when the seesaw brought you to the top and your friend to the bottom, and an instant later your friend was smiling at you from the top and you were on the bottom? It didn't matter whether you were up or down—it was all fun, all part of the seesaw. You didn't struggle to control which way the seesaw went—you just allowed the natural flow of this plaything to do what it was meant to do. It was the seesaw's job to move you up and down and, as long as there was someone opposite you, you would not fall and lose your balance. You didn't need to know exactly how that worked; you instinctively trusted that it would.

What would have happened if you had decided that you didn't trust the way the seesaw worked and you thought you had to somehow control it or figure it out in order for it to work properly? If you had made up your mind to jump off your end and go help your friend move her side up and down, your friend would have fallen to the bottom with a bang. The only thing the seesaw needed to maintain its natural flow, to work and stay in balance, was to have someone on either side of it allowing it to move up and down.

Balance, the element represented by the "B" in BLISS, is not about control or struggle. Balance is the free flow of energy that allows all people and things to move into the place they are meant to go, and it needs no help from us other than to maintain an equilibrium in our physical, mental, emotional, and spiritual bodies.

LOSING OUR BALANCE

When did the balance that came so naturally to us as children become such a struggle?

It started when we got off the seesaw at the park and climbed onto the seesaw of life. Life, like the seesaw, moves up and down, exactly as it is meant to. But suddenly, what was okay as a child wasn't okay as an adult. We started to *think* about our experiences rather than just *have* them. We stopped being with each moment and savoring each moment. We exchanged being in nature with being in thought. We exchanged simplicity for duplicity, fascination for infatuation. We began making judgments about what was good or bad, what was better or worse.

The moment we began to judge our experiences instead of just having them, we started to lose our balance. It happened when we began to measure our happiness or unhappiness by the external circumstances of our lives. We came to believe that our experiences define who we are, and we adopted a belief system constructed around our life experiences. We became more imbalanced as our perception of the physical universe, and ourselves, became entangled in a game of rejection or acceptance. We used to be delighted with ourselves, with our childhood antics, but as adults we focus on defending and justifying our actions to others.

Our imbalance became perpetual when we forgot that on the seesaw of life there is always Someone sitting on the other side: God. (When I say "God," I am referring to the Higher Power, the Universe, the Divine, or whatever name you choose for the Mother/Father Soul, the One Spirit.) We often forget that we are spiritual beings having a human experience, meaning that before we arrived here on planet Earth, we were residing elsewhere with others. Just because our souls decided to take up residency here on Earth does not mean that the others—God, our angels, guides, and teachers in the unseen—have forsaken us.

When I moved from Michigan to Arizona, the friends that I had made over the years didn't disappear from my life. I had only changed locations. They were still with me even if I didn't physically see them. They were in my heart and in my mind and were always there if I just wanted to chat or really needed them. It is no different with God, or our angels, guides, and teachers in the unseen. They always have been and always will be with us. It's not that they have forgotten us; we have forgotten them. We think that we are doing this earth assignment alone or only with those people we can physically see. That is simply not so. "As above, so below." We can regain our balance when we put the pieces of this truth back together, or "re-member" this truth.

When we consider the miracles that have happened in our lives or that we have witnessed in the lives of others, we are awed by the experience. In the realm of the unseen, miracles are normal everyday actions taken on our behalf. Some miracles seem larger than others, and they are what remind us that there is Someone out there paying attention to us. There are actually many looking out for us, and they appreciate and love it when we are aware of them.

If we were living our lives with the consciousness we had when we observed the ladybug on our arm, we would see what we call miracles every day of our lives. There would be no doubt in our minds that we are supported from a place that is not visible to the naked eye but is known within the heart. The more we nurture and understand our relationships with those in the unseen, the more we weave the tapestry of our very existence into a grander expression of our chosen life. Thus we create a balance between the seen and the unseen. If we didn't nurture the relationships we have with our friends on Earth, they would soon seem to disappear out of our lives. Whatever we don't pay attention to *appears* to cease existing.

There are many dimensions in the Universe. We live only on the third rung of this multidimensional ladder. We, as third-dimensional humans, who have actually been designed to have multidimensional experiences, have stopped paying attention to those things we can't taste, touch, smell, feel, or hear. That is what has led us to a belief system that we are down here doing everything on our own.

As adults, in every part of our interaction with life—our personal relationships, our working environments, our partnerships, our children, our social lives—we tend to believe that in order for anything to work, we alone are the ones who have to do something to fix it.

Can you recognize how difficult we have made it for ourselves? We are constantly waging war against some condition in our lives, and we resist the natural currents of life. When I was in my twenties, I saw a greeting card that read: "It's me against the world—I wonder who will win?" I bought it for myself because at the time that's how I felt. The sad thing is the card actually made me feel powerful. I believed I was so strong I could take on anything and win! Earth is not a jungle we're visiting in order to learn survival techniques. It is a temporary homestead where we have come to remember our ability to thrive—and, in spite of all the odds, through innocent perception and compassionate service, to be the purest form of love.

Surviving requires great effort, while thriving is the result of simply allowing. We rarely encounter any aspect of our day without manipulating, evaluating, coercing, or figuring out how to do it better or differently. Over and over again, we try to solve problems with the same mind that created the problems. As a result, there is rarely a day without emotional and mental upheaval. When we evaluate life through the prism of the mind, we don't understand the magnitude of our interference. The repercussions are astounding and set us back years in the growth of the soul (the soul is the Divine Spark of Life that is our essential nature).

LETTING GO

The following story speaks volumes about the value of balance in life and of letting go of trying to run your life with your mind.

18

In the late 1800s, there was a man in New York named Mr. Taylor. He sold clothing in the garment district of New York— not in a store, but from movable racks on the street in an area called the garment district. Month after month and year after year, hot weather or cold weather, Mr. Taylor showed up with his wonderful clothing, great attitude, and fair pricing. He was on the street selling his garments six days a week, and on the seventh, you would find him in church. Everyone loved Mr. Taylor.

As Mr. Taylor began to age, one of his dear old friends suggested he move into a store and sell his wares from there. "The weather is too much for you, my friend," he said. "It would be much easier if you worked from inside a store."

Mr. Taylor was uncertain about making such a move because he knew nothing about running a business indoors. He knew it would be much more involved than just taking the racks out of his van in the morning and putting them back at night. One very cold winter day, however, his friend's suggestion won out.

Mr. Taylor found a small store and began running his business the same way he did while on the street. He named his store "Taylor's." He still purchased wonderful clothes, asked a fair price, and was always kind to his customers. Yet within three months, Mr. Taylor realized he was losing money and feeling stress in the very business he had loved for so many years. Upon discussion with his friend, Mr. Taylor decided he needed a partner. He wasted no time taking one on.

Each morning Mr. Taylor had a meeting with his business partner. He wrote down everything that he knew how to do and he committed to doing these things every single day. The things he didn't know how to do well, he gave to his partner on a "to do" list. He promised to stay out of his partner's way, although he was used to controlling everything. He knew he needed to surrender what he did not know and focus on what he knew well.

At the end of each day, Mr. Taylor reviewed the day's events with his partner. Within six months, business was flourishing. Mr. Taylor was amazed at the number of people that were flocking to his store. He was in total joy! He had time to spend with his family and life was now back in balance. With his new success, he needed a larger store. And so he moved. In the process of opening the new location, he had a great desire to change the name of the store to include the name of his partner, who had made all the difference in his world. When the store opened, it bore its new name, "Lord and Taylor," and went on to become one of the most famous department stores in the world. When Mr. Taylor took on a partner, he took on the best: God.

INNER EXPLORATION

1. Write a letter of gratitude to yourself for all the hard work you have done this past year in making things happen the way you thought you wanted them to happen. Write down what it took for you to accomplish what you did, what sacrifices you made. Write down the obstacles yet to be overcome.

2. When you finish, write down what you would have delegated to a partner you trusted if you'd had one in this past year. How do you believe that would have changed your life?

3. Take on your partner! You know who that partner is. Enjoy the dance.

~~~~~

THERE ARE NO PROBLEMS—ONLY EXPERIENCES

As we become more enlightened, we learn to view what we call a problem as simply another experience, another part of life, which releases us from fixating on the need to solve the problem. This does not mean that we are not responsible in dealing with difficult situations we encounter; it only means that we are not always meant to figure out, interpret, or judge the experience.

The human mind is limited in its perception of outcomes. The moment we look to the mind to solve a problem, the mind sees an opportunity to create further aspects of the problem as the solution. It is the mind that creates problems, and we cannot solve a problem at the level that it was created.

The Mind of God encompasses unlimited outcomes, many of which we could never conceive or believe. How many times have you had an experience (or what you might call a problem) with an outcome that surprised you? If your answer is "rarely," then you tug and pull at a problem for so long that no result can happen other than the one you predict. If your answer is "often," it means you have not pondered to death the known possibilities (taken the life out of them), and instead have allowed yourself to be pleasantly surprised at the outcome. Most of us are not comfortable with uncertainty, so we are always looking for a solution and interrupting the balance of life when we were meant to experience its ebbs and flows.

Consider the Ocean

The ocean is a place where most of us experience pleasure and relaxation. We feel nurtured by the sound of the waves and refreshed by the feel of the water. It relaxes us and exhilarates us at the same time. Think about the tides. They rise and fall, again and again. There are times when the tides are rough due to weather conditions but the rhythm is always there. It's part of the ocean.

Every day in some part of the ocean, a dolphin swims, and in another part of the ocean, a shark glides. There are times when a boat sails upon the ocean's surface, cutting through the glistening waves, and other times when scuba divers descend into its depths to marvel at the rich, undersea life it hosts. People frolic in the water, and when nature calls, they may urinate in it. An oilrig may have a mishap and spill its inky cargo into the ocean's body. The setting sun uses the ocean as a canvas to display its magnificent colors—purples, pinks, oranges, and yellows. Cloudy skies turn the ocean's waters gray. While the ocean has many experiences—gentle tides and rough tides, changing colors, the arrival of foreign substances, and sharks and dolphins swimming in it simultaneously—it is always the ocean experiencing itself as the ocean.

The ocean is a meaningful metaphor for a life of balance: to still be (and be still) in the center of our emotions that rise and fall like the tides, and to hold ourselves steady when one day we feel surrounded by sharks and another day exhilarated by the nearness of dolphins. Balance is the place where no matter what kind of day we are having, or whether we are touched positively or negatively by people we encounter, we are still who we are, much like the ocean. There will never be a day in our human existence that does not carry diverse experiences, just as there will never be a day when the ocean does not host both dolphins and sharks.

So why is it that the experiences of a day or the people that participate in it, emotionally throw us either against the rocks or on the gentle back of the sand? Why is it that we seem unable to stay balanced through our experiences? Why do we let people and experiences define how we feel about our lives and ourselves? Perhaps it is because when we were growing up, no one ever taught us that our experiences do not define who we are.

The ocean is not the sharks and dolphins that swim in it. The creatures are just one of many aspects of the ocean but they don't define what it is. The ocean is not even the tide that moves its waters. Tides are one experience of the ocean and, not unlike us, the consciousness of the ocean is aware of that. The ocean doesn't turn on itself because it was urinated in. The ocean doesn't reject itself because an oil spill endangered its wildlife or made one part of it less beautiful than another. The ocean doesn't lose its balance because of its experiences. And we humans don't judge, reject, stop loving, or feel less peaceful in the presence of the ocean as a result of the experiences it has had. Instead, we travel many miles to be near and be soothed by the ocean, and many of us expend great effort in working to preserve the ocean.

Consider the Human

Our emotions, like the tides, will always rise and fall. There are days when we encounter kind, loving, compassionate people, and days we feel dumped on. We can look in the mirror on any given day and decide we look great, and other days decide we don't. We have our days of calm waters and days of roaring storms. Each of our days contains experiences, because it is through experiences that we meet and perceive life. Life would not be life without experiences. It is experience that supports the balance of life.

The only difference between the ocean and us is what we think. We humans knock ourselves off balance with our dispositions, attitudes, and assessments of our experiences. We take our experiences personally, without understanding the wisdom and the perfection of each experience. We experience a bad relationship, or perhaps several, and we believe we are unlovable. We experience the failure of a business and we believe we are unsuccessful. When someone (or several someone's) let us down in the past, we tend to misinterpret the words and actions of all others. If our father left when we were small, we may carry the belief that all men will leave us. If we were sexually abused as a child, we grow up mistrustful and prepared to protect ourselves from being hurt by those we have yet to meet. How we judged an experience ten years ago dictates how we will judge a related experience ten years from now. In other words, we are unable to have a fresh experience because our life is tainted by our thoughts of the past and all that we have not let go. Not letting go keeps us out of balance.

When the ocean experiences a tide, be it high or low, there is only one thing that happens—the waves merge, hit the shore, and disappear. The ocean has had the experience of that particular tide; it's over, and the ocean knows there will always be other tides, high or low, forceful or gentle. There is "no-thing" to react to—it is only an experience.

Zen Master Joshua, born in China in 778, was nearing death at the age of 120. His students gathered around their dying master and one said, "Master, please don't leave us without telling us the meaning of life." The Master smiled lovingly at his student and replied, "What's hot is hot, and what's cold is cold!" This was his way of saying what is, is.

The same consciousness, or God, that created the ocean also created us. The mind that we humans were given with which to think was never meant to be the bane of our existence. It was intended for us to use in harmony with the consciousness that created us, to assist us in reaching mastery or enlightenment.

With no need to think, the ocean has the freedom never to judge or make up its mind about the experiences it has. The ocean's lack of thought, and the special energy that it has as a result, is what reaches out to us and beckons us to its shores to relax our minds, our bodies, and our spirits. It brings us into balance. We receive from the ocean its very essence, which reflects back to us our very essence—the freedom just to be. The reason that we feel so peaceful when we are at the ocean is that everything is truly one consciousness. We merge our consciousness with that of the ocean and become one, or peace itself.

INNER EXPLORATION

1. Choose a place of stillness and beauty to do this meditation. Take seven slow, deep breaths. Inhale deeply, hold each breath for a moment, and then slowly exhale.

2. Envision yourself sitting on the warm sand on the shore of the ocean. With eyes closed and body relaxed, breathe in deeply the smell of the ocean. Feel the gentle breeze passing over your face. Feel the warmth of the sun's rays as they caress your body. Listen to the sounds you may hear at the ocean—waves lapping at the shore, seagulls calling. Completely relax into the feeling of sitting near the ocean.

3. Now go one step further and imagine that you are the ocean itself—without thought, with only the feeling of being merged with the consciousness of the ocean. Stay in this place until all of you has become one with the wisdom of the ocean. You will know this is so when you feel stillness throughout your body and silence within your mind. When you are ready, come back to the present. You will be aware that your breath has become a gentle rhythm that allows for life to simply be, your footsteps are lighter, your shoulders feel freer, and a gentle smile has found its way to your mouth.

4. The feeling of peaceful poise that is the wisdom
   of the ocean is always available to you. Whenever you have an experience and feel pulled to
   react to it or be defined by it, think of how you
   felt when you were merged with the ocean.

~~~~~~~

Freedom and peace come to us when we are able to have an experience and not be moved to judge it, or call it anything. We just have the experience, observe it, and seek the opportunity it contains, understanding that what transpires is not who we are, but only an experience we are having in order to gain wisdom and insight. Every single experience is designed to help us awaken to the truth of who we are, not carry on the illusion of who we have perceived ourselves to be.

Swami Kripalvanadri spoke profound words when he said to one of his students, "My beloved child, break your heart no longer. Each time you judge yourself, you break your own heart."

Experience is how life is lived and how the soul grows. Wisdom and knowledge come from experience. Instead of going into manic highs or depressed lows in reaction to the experiences of our lives, we must learn just to have them. What I have found of great value in helping me do this is to turn to my higher self, or to the God of my knowing, and ask, "What do I need to know from this experience? I attracted this experience to me—what is the opportunity here for my soul's growth?" I then become still and wait for the answer to be revealed.

Just asking that question will lead you toward emotional balance and greater clarity. It will also allow your energy to go where it is meant to go, instead of being diverted to the mind. The mind responds from a place of fear, acting out in anger, revenge, or betrayal. Asking the question of your higher self does not mean denying your feelings about the experience. Your feelings are important, and feelings that have been buried alive will never die. Asking the question will take you beyond your negative thoughts and judgments, which were created because of something that happened to you in the past. A past experience can energize the present with poison. Asking what you can learn disempowers that negative charge and restores balance.

A BLESSING IN DISGUISE

The following experience released once and for all a tie that I had to the past, and showed me how that tie had been affecting my present. This deeply painful experience was truly a blessing in disguise.

Sheila, an employee of mine, became a close friend. I knew that the circumstances under which we met and how she came to work for me had been orchestrated from the unseen. Early in our acquaintance, I became aware that we were mirrors for each other. She reflected aspects of myself that I wasn't particularly fond of, and some that I was. I was the same kind of mirror for her. Since I am aware that each person who enters my life comes bearing gifts, I was open to receiving this experience without judgment. She didn't understand it on the same level, but she knew there was more to our employer-employee relationship than met the eye.

Knowing in my heart that this was an agreement between souls destined to meet at this particular time, I hired her even though I could not comfortably afford her salary. We worked out an agreeable part-time arrangement with a commitment that, within a three-month period, she would become a full-time employee with her desired salary and benefits. I honored that agreement even though at the time it was financially very difficult for me. Twice she quit, and twice I took her back because that voice, that precious voice inside me, guided me to. My mind, reflecting my old pattern, would have done the exact opposite. I didn't know why, but it felt necessary for me to continue with Sheila.

Working with each other in the beginning was not necessarily easy for either one of us. I was used to doing things the way I thought they should be done in order to achieve a particular result. She did things completely differently. She also did things very well. When we hit bumps in the road, I would spend whatever time was necessary to work through with her what we needed to in order to move forward. I always listened to her perspective and she to mine. We both gained a lot from the relationship. There was never a time when she was in a personal crisis that I didn't find a way to help her. There were occasions when, long after business hours, we were still talking things over at nine or ten o'clock at night. At times it almost seemed as if the requirements of this relationship were like those of a marriage!

There came a time after a few months when the differences between us didn't matter any more. Our lengthy discussions to get over the bumps were no longer necessary, and I came to love Sheila like a sister. She once made the comment that if she worked for me for free, she would still be compensated by all she had learned. I was grateful that her presence had taught me so much about myself, and I was grateful to myself that I was open to learning more about myself through her. I took her on a shopping spree for Christmas, and she shared the Christmas holiday with my family of friends and me. I thought we would work together for years to come.

The new year arrived. I implemented new office policies and gave Sheila a $5,000 raise. She entered the new year with a new boyfriend who was very wealthy, affording her more financial opportunities than I could at that time. She adopted a different attitude toward our work and me. She rebelled against office policies and felt she had earned the right to pretty much come and go as she pleased. It was clear that the tide was about to turn. Knowing her as well as I did, I was aware that money and opportunity motivated her. I also knew that "being taken care of" was what gave her a sense of security. She began hinting at her resignation. When she did resign, I wasn't surprised, but I was blindsided by the manipulative, dishonest, and calculating behavior that she engaged in on her way out. There is no need to go into the details, but suffice it to say that it was a complete turnaround from the Sheila I thought I knew.

My first feeling was a painful sense of betrayal that immediately brought to mind the image of my mother and stepmother. These two women were strongly associated with deep betrayal in my past. My stepmother's face layered over that of Sheila and it shook me to the core. I thought I had moved past the betrayal by my mother and stepmother. I was wrong. The pain in the center of my heart was deep and it felt old. I knew this pain was caused by more than this current experience, so I sat down four days later on a Saturday morning, turned to God, and prayed, "Dear God, give me the wisdom to understand what I need to learn from this experience."

It took all my strength not to see myself as the victim in this experience and, consequently, to make Sheila wrong. It's much easier to take things personally and make someone else wrong, so we don't have to look at our contribution to the experience. It takes great courage to talk to ourselves truthfully. It took everything I had ever taught any client or spoken about to any group to remind me that I was not the victim and, no matter what it looked like, I had drawn this experience to me. I sat with my prayer for hours, crying off and on from that old, deep place in my heart. I didn't do anything to distract myself from the prayer or my desire to see what I needed from this experience. I didn't leave my house. I calmed my mind and loved myself enough to wait patiently for the answer to come. On Sunday, the answer began to emerge. It was all about the betrayal baggage I hadn't realized I was still carrying.

I had done a great deal of inner healing, diligently and vigilantly, through the years. I had peeled back, like an onion, so many layers of feelings over so much time, it seemed incredible that this thick layer of pain could still be there. The Universe, in all its wisdom, knew that this layer was key to where I was going next. And so the perfect experience that I needed to "get it" was brought forward at exactly the right time in my life—in the form of an employee. I now had the emotional tools not only to get through this experience, but also to understand it on the deepest levels where it was meant to be understood. Only then could I release it.

I was moved that Sunday evening to write in my journal. Journaling for me is one way to reach past the mind and allow higher wisdom to come through. It's a practice that has become as essential to me as eating. I opened my journal, picked up my pen, and wrote:

"Dear God,

I feel like I've been run over by a bus. I'm feeling great sadness and fear about how things will be with Sheila gone. I counted on her and depended on her for so much. I can't imagine BLISS [the name of my company] without her. I feel very betrayed, but I know this is not *about Maureen being betrayed. I really choose to move away from what this looks like and be at peace with the truth, whatever that may be. In spite of what has just happened, I feel very blessed by you, God, and all of my angels, guides, and teachers. What a blessing to feel that love in the midst of this storm. Thank you for sending me Neal [a new friend] on the same day that Sheila left. Neal is another angel, who appeared out of the blue to help me, to love me, to just be there for me while I work this one out. It really is true that when a door shuts, a window opens. That happened very quickly. I know in the very depths of my soul that not only will things be okay, they will be great, even though right now I feel very hurt and confused."*

Then, in the silence, I heard, and my pen wrote of its own volition:

"You will thrive, my child, not merely survive."

"God, I wrote Sheila a letter, venting my feelings about everything, but I have not decided whether to mail it."

"Do you want to be right, or do you want to be happy?" asked God.

"I'm not looking to be right, God, I'm just thinking maybe my part was to break her vicious pattern.

"This is not about her, Maureen, this is about you, for you. You have carried with you a sense of betrayal since you were a child. Your belief that someone has betrayed you is *your* truth, not *the* truth. What you call betrayal is your judgment of an experience. You are still judging the behavior of others, although you have come a long way. No one has ever betrayed you. Every experience of what you call betrayal happens so you can come to understand your own judgments about right and wrong. There have been times in your life when others interpreted your behavior as betrayal. Yet your intention was not to betray anyone. That was their truth about the situation. Had they confronted you with their belief that you betrayed them, you would have been astounded because you wouldn't have seen it that way. What you call betrayal is only a judgment formulated in your mind about someone else's behavior in a particular circumstance. Do you understand this?"

I took this information into my heart and pondered it for a while before I responded.

"Yes, I do. And I know that up until this point in my journey I never could have understood it on this level. Once again, I have been lifted up. Even the sadness has been lifted. Truth is so much better than fiction. Writing is an amazing thing, God, and the process of discovering truth is exciting, although at times quite daunting. It's such a wonderful feeling to know that I have so much support in the visible world as well as in the invisible. I wish everyone could understand the process of life and your role in it, as well as the roles of the angels, guides, and teachers. I love you, God."

"I love you, my child. Get some rest and then enjoy nature this week. Air out, have fun, breathe in life. Don't hold your breath."

And so the experience passed. I gave thanks for it, which is not to say that I would choose to have Sheila in my life again, or that I would be sending her Christmas cards, but I blessed her. Without her, I would still be carrying around the baggage marked "Betrayal," and part of my life would still be very much out of balance.

INNER EXPLORATION

1. Choose one of your "zinger" issues, something that has been plaguing you and that you know is keeping you off balance. It may be what you label in the behavior of others as betrayal or abandonment of you, dishonesty or manipulation, being controlling, or even promiscuity. Your zinger issue might be victimhood, with you falling prey to any of the above. Write down your zinger of choice. If several issues come up, write them all down, but focus on just one for now.

2. Direct your attention to the center of your heart and feel your love there. If you feel like crying, go ahead. Crying washes the soul and helps remove built-up sludge and debris from the inside out. Now, from the center of your heart, feel the weight of your particular issue. Stay with it and feel it. Acknowledge that it is there.

3. Write down as many circumstances as you can remember that took place in this past year related to your particular issue—experiences whose divine purpose was to get your attention, but in which you may have placed yourself in the victim role.

4. Now, be present with the God of your knowing, or the highest part of yourself, and ask, "What do I need to know about this from the wisdom

of time, that I may be able to change my role from victim to beneficiary of opportunity?"

5. Stay with this question until you have an answer that comes from a place higher than your ego or mind. Stay with it, write about it, cry about it, get angry about it, feel it, but don't allow yourself to be distracted. Write pages, write for hours, or write for days, whatever it takes. Don't stop until you begin to gain clarity without anger or you'll miss the gift. At this point you may not get the entire picture, but you will have opened a pinhole that will grow wider and brighter with time and your attention. Don't judge anything. Allow for higher wisdom to enter when the mind has quieted.

6. When you understand the zinger, you can remove this particular piece of baggage from your collection. Bless it and all that accompanied it and let it go.

With this technique you can begin to remove the barriers of your past experiences and know that your future is created by your thoughts and convictions. In all your experiences from this day forward, you can call forth compassion and understanding and know that the Universal Mind, or ALL THAT IS, will not bring you any experience that will not be a gift to establish your balance and propel you forward— unless you decide otherwise.

~~~~~~

EAST MEETS WEST: SUPPORTING BALANCE

Our gifts come from every relationship we have. In any relationship between two people, balance exists as two distinct entities vibrating at their own rates, and yet finding a point where they merge or emerge in harmony.

Eastern wisdom embraces the idea that human beings are born in bliss, are held in bliss during their lifetime, and transcend to bliss after leaving the earth. We are here to walk in the light of a truth that moves far past any truth the mind presently knows. There is only one reason that we are here on this planet: for the soul to grow, through love for others and for ourselves. The soul struggles to grow when we are out of balance with our feelings, our heart, or our love.

Through love and patience, the Eastern philosophies teach, we will transcend the illusion of separation. The teachings lead us further into the wisdom that we don't have to improve ourselves, just simply let go of what blocks our hearts. They remind us that when we look into the eyes of another, we remember there is no separation, only the rhythm of giving and receiving, teaching and learning. The only difference between us is our personal preferences and what we are accustomed to. Each person we meet is a reflection of our own individuality. Each person gives us the opportunity to come into balance because, to return to the playground metaphor, the "see would not saw" without both parts.

Western culture, on the other hand, has groomed us to think about ourselves. Self-preservation! What *we* need, what *we* want, what *we* have to do in order to succeed. We have not been taught to love ourselves and others. Darwin's theory, "survival of the fittest," forms the basis of much of Western culture, and what a tragedy that is! Western culture has taught us how to judge, not to accept. It has taught us that *this* is better and *that* is worse. It has made competition a national sport. We have learned to focus on comparing ourselves with others, and this sense of duality has encouraged our imbalance. It is in this comparison that the truth of the soul is negated, and the only reason we are here—to express love to each other and ourselves—is diminished.

We have been led to believe that the fitness of our bodies signifies status, when the purpose of the body is to host the soul during its experience of growth on this planet. Our bodies are to be honored and cared for because they play such an important role in the soul experience, not for the shape or size of breasts and butts. We have been taught incorrectly about why we are here on Earth, and we continue to foster this incorrect notion in ourselves and to teach it to our unsuspecting children—who then become out-of-balance adults.

This is not to say we don't bless and give thanks to all those in our lives who did the best they could with what they knew to teach us and tell us. Perhaps they didn't know how to teach us about our feelings and emotions, our hearts and souls. Perhaps they didn't know there was a difference between living life from your head or coming from your heart. Perhaps they weren't aware that false perceptions about everything around us and about ourselves would create an imbalance not only in us, but also on the very planet we inhabit. Perhaps they didn't remember the truth about God, the angels, the guides, and the teachers—so they didn't have it to teach us.

We may have had no one in our lives to tell us we could have an experience, look at it, not judge it, see what we needed to learn from it, still not judge, and then let it go, simply let it go. Those who shaped our beliefs probably didn't know there is another way to define one's self besides through the thoughts and opinions of other people. They probably didn't know that there is another way to live besides struggling to look important in the eyes of society (whoever that is) and be accepted, even though we believe ourselves to be unacceptable.

RETURNING TO BALANCE

Now it is our responsibility to regain our lost balance by discovering the wisdom of our heart and the knowledge of our soul. We must heal the wounded mind and dispel the myth about who we are, so we may come to the truth of our authentic nature. It doesn't matter where we've come from, it only matters where we're going. We have blamed our past, our ancestors, our mothers, fathers, lovers, husbands, and wives long enough. Nobody is listening anymore, except us. The baggage we have carted with us for all these years is with us only because we think it is. We are not our baggage. We may have thought it was helpful for our personal agendas, and it may have been at one time, but it doesn't work anymore—not for us and not for anyone else. Now is the time to move from the head down into the heart.

INNER EXPLORATION

1. Prepare to write by first surrounding yourself with what you love. You can write outdoors in nature or in a bathtub encircled by candles. You can write after going through favorite pictures of friends and family, or after watching your precious pet saunter through the room. The important thing is, before you begin writing, to surround yourself with what feels good to you.

2. Now pause and take in what you love. Whatever touches your heart, feel it, breathe into it, expand it. Focus on your heart. See the color pink surrounding your heart and then expanding throughout your body and into the very corners of your mind. Feel the energy of your heart. Touch your heart and feel its beat. Feel its love for you.

3. Spend whatever time you need to truly connect with your heart.

4. Then write a letter to yourself dictated by your heart. It will be a love letter because the heart knows only love. Ask your heart to tell you the truth about you. Ask your heart to tell you what you have forgotten about your precious self and ask your heart what it needs from you. The let-

ter might be long, and that will be wonderful—more love from your heart to you! Your mind has already taken up most of your time and has told you enough for now. Your heart has a new message for you. Receive it.

5. Once you have translated the message from your heart onto paper, put it next to your bed so it will be the first thing you see when you wake up in the morning and the last thing you see at night. Honor it. The message of the heart will begin to bring you into balance. Balance is achieved when you quiet the mind long enough to hear the music of the heart—and then the mind and the heart can have their waltz.

Our life experiences are not meant to keep us in a state of imbalance and unrest. Our experiences are meant to make an impression on us so that when the time is right, we will remember our true nature and long to return to it. If we don't receive those impressions, we won't know there is something to return to. If we don't let go of some things along the way, there will be no space to celebrate a newly emerging stage of life. If we don't experience being out of balance, we won't know how necessary balance is for inner peace and for the relationship with ourselves and others. The only way for the soul to grow is to experience and accept chaos. Out of chaos always comes order if we understand the balance of life and allow that outcome to be expressed. If there were only order, how would we grow? What would we appreciate? Where would wisdom come from?

Our great accomplishment in life is meant to be more than just skating on its icy surface and trying to keep our balance. We are meant to go ice fishing in the lake of ourselves, where the depth is unfathomable and the catches are endless. If we do this work, then our ice skating can turn into ice dancing, where we no longer struggle to keep our balance but become balance itself. In balance we have the ability to go beyond our day-to-day understanding and tap into the wisdom of the ages.

Balance is the beginning of bliss.

CHAPTER 2

Love

*Dear God, starting today, help us to love ourselves so much
that we never set up any circumstances that go against us.*
—Don Miguel Ruiz

One of the most thought-provoking questions you can
ask yourself is: Am I loved and do I love well? I've asked
that question of many people and the majority answered, "I
think so." To *think* so is tragic, to *know* so, magic. The pri-
mary purpose of life is to live it in a state of love. To live life
in a state of love is to live your life led by your heart. When
we live life with love, we are gifted with peace and a sense of
oneness with all of life.

If you only *think* that you are loved, some part of you is
taken up with the belief that you are not loved. If you only
think that you love well, some part of you is taken up with
the belief that you do not love well. This translates into duality, separation, and a mind and heart both divided and
disconnected from that which is all loving: God. If you only
think you are loved or only think you love well, feelings of

malnourishment will leave you angry, frustrated, jealous, sad, and frightened. The presence of these emotions is a good barometer of your answer to the question of whether you are loved and love well.

To know that you are loved is not only to know that others love you, but also to know that you love yourself. To experience real love and to be genuinely loved is to live your life with the commitment and understanding that the requirements of the personality are secondary to the need to regard yourself and others with loving compassion. Love, when fully expressed, relinquishes fear, self-doubt, and the need to have what you give be given back to you.

In making a half-hearted attempt to love ourselves or another, trying to hang on to what we think is love or trying to prove we are loving by occasional loving acts only results in struggle. Struggle is inevitable when we allow the mind to devise plans for love, rather than letting our hearts do what comes naturally. Love is much deeper than the content of our thoughts. Letting our thoughts try to run love creates a hole for fear to creep in and blindness to the truth to take over. Contained within fear are guilt, worthlessness, blame, and negativity. Wherever love is not known, our thoughts attack us and only confirm to us that we are not worthy of love.

In the moment that we still our thoughts, love rises and fear subsides. **Love**, the "L" in our acronym BLISS, is where we continue our journey. Since love is our true nature, struggling with love as we often do—in the giving of it, the hanging on to the impression of it, or the receiving of it—is unnatural. Your life is supremely important and deserving of *your* love. When you come to know how to love yourself well—how to accept yourself, be gentle with yourself, forgive yourself, nurture yourself, speak kindly to yourself, be okay with not being okay with yourself—you will come to know how to love another, and love well. In every moment that you touch your own heart, you become well acquainted with love and receive the recipe for loving another.

To know that you are loved and to know that you love well takes you far beyond thought to an internal place of the soul that merely watches thoughts come and go. If you notice how love finds its way from inside you to another person, you can feel it move from within your soul, down the corridor to your heart, and expand outward from your heart center. Similarly, when another loves you, you can feel that love coming to you from the center of that person's heart. You can think of that center as the delicious soft center of a piece of mouthwatering chocolate. Once you reach the center, you savor it slowly, so you can experience its flavor fully.

Love is effortless, magical, and transforming. Love comes from such a deep place that it often brings us to tears with its impact. What it really brings us to is Oneness with God—with all living breathing life—as it was always intended to do. What once was ordinary becomes extraordinary and holy. Love is a feeling so fulfilling and so unifying that we shed joyful tears. Symbolically, the shedding of these tears is the shedding of a veil that has kept us separate from this Oneness, this love.

ASK THE CHILDREN

So how do we distinguish between *thinking* we are loved and loving others well to *knowing* that we are? How do we recognize love in our lives? The definition of love is elusive to many. While many consider it an outside force subject to the conditions of daily life, it is not. As adults, we tend to overanalyze the question "What is love?" and struggle to come up with the "right" answer. The right answer is simple—just ask the children.

Billy, age four, said, "When someone loves you, the way they say your name is different. You know that your name is safe in their mouth."

Karen, age seven, said, "When you love somebody, your eyelashes go up and down and little stars come out of you."

Rebecca, age eight, said, "When my grandmother got arthritis, she couldn't bend over and paint her toenails anymore. So my grandfather does it for her all the time, even though his hands have arthritis, too. That's love."

Mark, age seven, said, "When my little sister pulls my hair, I give her a big bear hug and start to tickle her. Then I give her a kiss. Even though she says 'yuck,' she starts to giggle. I know she likes that."

Sara, age five, said, "Love is when my family goes out to have ice cream and I let my daddy have a lick of my ice-cream cone because I know he likes it."

Abby, age four, said, "When my mommy comes and tucks me in at night before I go to sleep, I know she loves me."

Mary Ann, age four, said, "Love is when your puppy licks your whole face even when you've left her alone all day."

Nicole, age eleven, said, "Love is when you've had an argument with your best friend and you call her up at night and say I love you."

Karl, age five, said, "Love is when a girl puts on perfume and a boy puts on cologne and then they tell each other how good they smell."

Bobby, age seven, said, "Love is when Grandma and Grandpa hug while everyone's looking."

Jessica, age eight, said, "Love is when Mommy gives Daddy her favorite part of the chicken."

Bobby, age ten, said, "Love is what's in the room with you at Christmas if you stop opening presents and listen."

All of these children are clear about what love is, and they answer naturally, from their hearts. The following story illustrates love in action. A friend of mine told me the story, and then I read it in Marc Gafni's book *Soulprints*.

Many years ago, the Seattle Special Olympics hosted nine contestants, all physically or mentally challenged. The nine contestants practiced long and hard for the moment in time when they knew that one of them would be the winner. They positioned themselves at the starting line for the hundred-yard dash.

The gun went off, and they all started out with great exuberance. But, moments after he began, one small boy stumbled on the asphalt. He burst into tears.

The other eight contestants heard the boy crying. They all slowed down and looked behind them to see what had happened. They stopped, and then every single one of them went back to help the young boy in distress. Every single one of them.

One little girl, who had Down's syndrome, bent over and kissed the little boy on his forehead. "This," she said, "will make you better." They all surrounded the young boy and helped him up. Arm in arm, all nine crossed the finish line together. The crowd stood and cheered for eight full minutes. These competitors had all won the race—together.

The most powerful message from this story is that each child in the competition responded to the cry for help with a natural impulse: selflessness. The future of our ability to love ourselves and others is dependent upon remembrance of our love in its truest and purest form—its natural state as it existed when we were children.

NATURAL VERSUS NORMAL

As adults, we tend to characterize our actions as "normal" behavior. "I can't help it, it's just the way I am!" is something we have all said to defend our nonconscious or unloving behaviors. We have forgotten or abandoned our natural selves. Love is a natural trail that leads us out of the ego's thicket of who we think we are into the clearing of who we know ourselves to be. Love is simple and exists without thought. Love is an automatic response to ourselves and others when not clouded by the conditioning of our past.

The children from the Seattle Special Olympics did what came naturally to them. All of them knew simultaneously and without thought or agenda that they were going back for the little boy and they would all finish the race together. Winning became the least important aspect of the experience, even though at one time the children believed it was the most important. Caring for the young boy became the paramount goal. The children's caring reflected who they were, and what they did was a by-product of their understanding. The beauty of that experience, called a race, was that all the adults in the stands and on the sidelines were able to witness a natural outpouring of love.

Adults in the same situation would perhaps have heard the faint cry of another, but their normal response would most likely have been to keep on going, to win the race, because that's what they believed they came to do. That's what they trained for and what their coaches groomed them for. Friends and family in the stands would be waiting for their runner to beat everyone else. "Win at all costs!" That is the normal behavior indoctrinated by a society that prides itself on competition, being "better than" rather than "being one with" another person.

It has become normal for us to think we know what a certain experience is meant to bring us. But that is not natural. That is cutting off the unlimited possibilities of any particular circumstance at any particular moment. It keeps us from the real intended prize.

The Angel in Fur

Like many of us, I have been blessed with numerous opportunities to realize that experiences presented to me most often have surprisingly different and loving results than I anticipate. I now know that I have the choice to enter an experience for the adventure and potential it offers, rather than attempting to control it or figure out the results beforehand. The following experience poignantly brought this awareness home to me.

About a year ago, I was hurrying out of my office to the rest room downstairs. My office at the time was on the second floor of a beautiful, Spanish hacienda–style office complex. My day had been extremely hectic and a bit tense, to say the least. I thought I would just be a minute, then be back with clients, paperwork, and phones without pause until around eight o'clock that night. As I came down the stairs, something prompted me to look up. There, between two large Spanish pillars, crouched a tiny gray kitten with two luminous green eyes boring through me. In that moment, time stopped, our eyes locked, and those eyes told me telepathically that we were about to have an experience together.

Heeding the message of those eyes, I agreed to have this experience, whatever it was.

I snapped back to the moment and realized that behind the eyes was a tiny kitten that must, I thought, belong to someone in the office building. Forgetting the demands waiting for me in my office, I went in pursuit of the kitten's owner. I first entered the leasing office, asking if anybody knew anything about this kitten. They all said "no," but commented that the cat had been spotted for the past two days at various locations around the office complex. I explained that this precious little kitten on the second floor was apparently lost and needed help.

The building's receptionist dropped what she was doing and began leafing through the yellow pages to find animal emergency or cat rescue. She let her voice mail answer the ringing phones. I went back out to retrieve the kitten, but she (or he) was gone. High heels clicking, I was in hot pursuit when the secretary who worked next door to me came out of her office and asked what I was doing. I explained, and she joined me in trying to find the elusive feline.

Down the outdoor sidewalks, from office building to office building, we scurried. We kept spotting the kitten from afar, but the creature was so incredibly fast that we couldn't keep up with it. Along the way, an attorney came out of his office, and I asked him if he would take another route and try to help us capture the kitten. I think he was stunned because we'd never met before, but he couldn't seem to say "no." With suit jacket and tie flapping in the wind, he ran off in another direction, looking for the kitten.

Soon I spotted the tiny ball of fur actually jumping onto the second-story roof. I paused for a second in amazement at its quickness and determination to keep the chase up, then I ran past a modeling agency two doors down from the roof that the kitten had landed on.

Three people came out—the owner and two women who worked there. I had never met any of these people either. One of the women was seven months' pregnant. They all joined the search-and-rescue team. There were now seven of us away from our offices, away from our normal routines, away from what we called important, clicking and flapping after this kitten. The only *thing that mattered was the rescue. What a ride this little cat was taking us on!*

The attorney caught up with us and jumped onto the rooftop to grab the kitten, only to see it run into a drainpipe, the other end of which opened onto a pile of rocks on the first floor. The woman who was seven months' pregnant ran into her office to get some turkey to try to encourage the kitten to come out, and then she actually climbed onto the roof by herself. I ran down to the ground floor, but by the time I got there, the cat had already gone through the drainpipe, apparently landed on the rocks, and was on its way again to another part of the building.

All seven of us spotted our quarry at almost the same time. The little animal was lodged behind a huge clay flowerpot. We surrounded the hiding place. Without one word, five of us backed away while the pregnant woman and her colleague grabbed the visibly shaken kitten.

Again, time stopped. I was standing breathless, tears rolling down my face, watching the oneness of us all. We all had one common goal: to save the kitten. We all stopped our normal routines to do what came naturally: to help someone in need (in this case, a kitten). With the kitten finally in the arms of the pregnant woman (who decided to keep her), the luminescent green eyes once again knowingly connected to mine. I knew in that moment that the kitten was the catalyst to bring all of us to a higher awareness of what in our "busy" day was most important.

This kitten was sent to our particular office complex to teach us about oneness, about love—not business, not busy-ness, not how many clients we could acquire, not our lofty positions—just pure love. In that moment, I fell in love with every one of those people who had stepped out of their normal routines and done what came naturally to them. I had already fallen in love with the kitten. I called her the "Angel in Fur." I fell in love with myself as well for listening to the unspoken words and, finally, I fell in love with love itself.

We all looked at each other. Thirty minutes before, we'd been complete strangers. Thirty minutes later, we were experiencing a great love for each other, including the kitten. We all walked away in complete silence, each of us taking away our own meaning of what had just occurred. Each of us was feeling the importance of the experience. I became even more aware that there is only One facilitating love for all of us. We are all one.

What keeps us from experiencing great love is usually what we regard as normal behavior, which is not natural behavior. Normal is what we *think* it is, whereas natural has no need for a particular perspective—it just is. Normal is doing-ness and natural is being-ness. When we allow things to occur naturally, we realize that the consciousness that brought us here—God, pure love, or All That Is—sustains us. This consciousness is with us, within us, of us, around us, and embraces us always.

Have you ever spent even one moment *thinking* your heart into beating or *thinking* your lungs into breathing? Did you ever once have to *think* your hair or nails into growing? Certainly not, but if you did think about it, you would realize that you never have to make a conscious effort for those things to occur. They happen naturally. It is the same with love. The Consciousness that brought us here also sustains us here—with love.

Love is the single most important power given to us from the beginning of time. It is the foundation of our relationship to the Universe and all of life, both seen and unseen. Love means accepting and connecting to all the experiences of our lives. Each experience that enters our lives is a fruit born of the Tree of Life and is intended to bring us closer to our true nature—love. It is through loving every experience, even those that appear to be dark, that we gain momentum and witness discordance transformed. Love is a dynamic living force. It is not a word. It is a power. It is life! Love's healing tenderness penetrates all conditions of life. Love restores, rebuilds, and rectifies. Life is love in action.

Love in action comes from *natural* behavior. Natural behavior arises from a place above thought, our nonlogical mind—the Mind of God. We have been taught that we must be logical. What does being logical mean but a complex, complicated attempt to figure something out that has no defined answer anyway, except in our minds? The nonlogical Mind of God maintains simplicity. The only question it asks is, as Neale Donald Walsch, author of *Conversations with God,* puts it, "What would love do now?"

Love must saturate our thoughts if our thoughts are going to have any value for our lives and contribute to creating balance. There is nothing that cannot be superseded, no injustice that cannot be brought into balance, when it is backed by the outpouring of love.

Morrie Schwartz (the Morrie of *Tuesdays with Morrie,* by Mitch Albom) said, "The most important thing in life is to learn how to give out love, and to let it come in. Love is the only rational act." Viewed in this light, what we consider normal behavior is not rational.

Normal behavior—what we think is right or wrong, good or bad, what we *have* to do, or how we *have* to act—comes from our thoughts about the past and our fears concerning the future. Normal behavior tends to have an agenda. Our normal behavior operates on self-preservation, while our natural behavior is fueled by love. Love gives the soul the freedom to experience the richness that it came here for.

Our belief that we must think about something in order for it to occur is both accurate and inaccurate. It is by our thoughts and only by our thoughts that we create. But what do we create? If thought is not supported by love—gentle wisdom from the soul and pure love from the heart—we create an imbalance. Love is the only true creative energy. Thought without the backing of love keeps us in the dark, and moves us away from enlightenment and into a vibration that surrounds us with doubt, fear, anger, and bitterness.

INNER EXPLORATION

1. Write down five things that you have done, thought, or said in the past month that you know were not loving, but which were in keeping with your *normal* way of perceiving and judging a situation. Be honest, and don't judge yourself. This is for your eyes only.

2. When you finish, reflect upon those five circumstances and from a place of pure love, pure heart, the *natural* place of your being, recreate each one of them. What would you have said, done, or thought differently? It's important to write this down.

3. Now, this may be the toughest part, but it is indeed the most important part. Recreate those situations once more in your mind's eye, starting from your *normal* behavior and ending with your *natural* behavior. This means going back to each situation and adjusting whatever is neces-

sary to interrupt the flow of your normal behavior and replace it with natural behavior. You will be blessed for having done this.

4. Now feel the difference!

The greatest thing that we can do for anyone in the world is a favor. This inner exploration is a favor you can do for yourself and indirectly for others. Make no mistake: love is an internal energy that comes from our true nature.

~~~~~~~~

To Love or Suffer

Far too often, we withhold love from ourselves and others because our past experiences lead us to fear being hurt again. There are as many reasons and stories for withholding love from ourselves and each other as there are people on this planet. The reasons for withholding love aren't important; creating love is. Thinking of love as something external related to the conditions of daily life invariably leads to conflict and suffering. Consider all the expectations we place on people and things to provide us with love and happiness. We expect it from our partners, our families, our friends, our pets, and our jobs. We expect that money and possessions will make us happy. When any or all of them don't fill us up the way we want them to (and they won't), we crash. We become disillusioned, disheartened, and depressed. We suffer! And others suffer as our disappointment creates conflict in our relationships.

The old definition of love vanishes when we come to understand that *love is who we are*. Take that in for a moment—it is important. *Love is who we are!* The ability to embrace that concept will bring great relief to us. Love is not based on the changing circumstances of our lives. Love is greater than any experience that life brings. Love is constant and eternal.

When we withhold our love because of conditions in our daily lives, we isolate ourselves in lonely retreat, licking our self-imposed wounds for years. In our relationships, we replay past betrayals and hurts, victimize ourselves, abandon ourselves, abandon others before they abandon us, all the while imagining a future without love or imagining a future with a perfectly intellectualized version of love. We manage to become both tedious in our angst and skilled architects in building our walls of protection.

What we are protecting ourselves from is life. We are here to participate in life, not to languish in past experiences of pain. Love is larger than pain. Pain is a manifestation of the mind that comes and goes. Love is an experience of the heart that, once realized, can never *not* be.

I have had numerous clients come to me over the years in great fear of opening their hearts to love for fear they will be overwhelmed, overpowered, and out of control. They say they cannot bear the thought of going through that much pain again, and my response is "Stop thinking!" Most people have never experienced a great love in their life because they have never experienced their own love for their own life.

We will never experience the love of another to a degree greater than the love we are able to give to ourselves. The measure of our past loves or current loves is in direct proportion to the love we give (or do not give) to ourselves.

One of my clients, Diane, came to me with great trepidation. She knew her life was going in painful circles, yet she was terrified, as she put it, "to open Pandora's box." She was forty-six, divorced, in the midst of a ten-year affair with a married man, and occasionally seeing an unmarried man, who was an alcoholic and lived three hours away from her. Both men were emotionally unavailable, both safe bets (she thought) because she said she "didn't want to have her heart broken again."

We began by doing a meditation to quiet her mind and lead her into the feelings of her heart. I asked her to listen to just one message her heart had to tell her, and she began to cry uncontrollably. When I asked her what she was feeling, she said, "I don't want to go there. I can't, it's too painful for me." Knowing the importance of honoring where she was in the moment, I was prompted to ask her if she had a heart necklace at home or something with hearts on it.

She reacted negatively. "I hate hearts. I don't have anything with hearts on it, and anytime someone gave me something with hearts on it, I threw it away." I wasn't surprised, because I realized that for her to look at a heart would evoke feelings for her own heart that she had shut down years before.

Since she had come to me for help, I asked if we could begin by attempting to get past an obvious point of resistance. I asked her to buy herself something, anything that had a heart on it or represented the heart, and to please bring it to our next session. She panicked, saying she didn't know what to get, asking me what she should get and where. I suggested she just allow herself to be led to the perfect heart for her. Cautiously, she said she would try.

I anticipated that she would come back the following week with the most minuscule heart she could find, just to pacify me with something. Much to my surprise, she came into my office with a big white box, the lid on tight. I asked her if she would show me what she'd brought. *She told me she hadn't opened the box since she'd first bought it, and then cautiously lifted the lid. What emerged was a magnificent eight-inch-high, ruby red, pure crystal heart. I looked at her and we both began to cry. When I asked her why she had chosen this particular heart, she told me that when she looked at it, it reminded her of the big heart she had always known was in her, but had long since locked away. She told me about the pain she'd felt in the past, beginning with her strict religious upbringing. No matter what she did as a child or as a young adult, her parents called her bad and told her God did not approve of her behavior. She felt worthless. She went on to marry a man who supported her belief in her worthlessness. She manifested in her outer world what she felt in her inner world. She felt she was bad and, consequently, drew bad circumstances into her life. With so much pain to bear, she shut down her heart.*

We put the crystal heart on the table between us and I proceeded to tell her how magnificent her own heart was and how it had missed her so much while she was away. She talked about how closed off her heart felt while having an affair with the man who would never leave his wife for her and the man who would never leave his alcohol for her. With my arms around her, supporting her, she wept her heart open.

After that, she kept the crystal heart on her nightstand so it would be the first thing she saw in the morning and the last thing she saw at night. She came to love that heart. In time she came to love her own heart. With great courage, she ended both relationships that were keeping her from her own love and from being truly loved, and began her journey to bliss.

We all had an imperfect childhood. We have all had lovers who wounded us to the core, and friends who broke our hearts. These experiences are part of our history. Each day, we are either loving or suffering, according to what we conceive, accept, and allow—now. We have two choices: learn to love and understand that love is our Divine birthright, and therefore the essence of who we are, or continue to suffer in the delusion that love capriciously darts in and out of our daily lives.

INNER EXPLORATION

1. Buy yourself a heart—one that you feel truly represents your heart. If you already have one and you love it, then use that. If not, there are many to choose from. Perhaps a solid gold heart, or a teddy bear with a soft cuddly heart that a child would play with, maybe a purple amethyst heart, or a whimsical heart. It could be a crystal heart, a pink quartz heart, or a handblown glass heart. One of my clients bought me a heart that was smooth on one side and rough on the other and hung from a gold stand. It was meant to represent life—the smooth and the rough. My favorite heart is a wall sculpture I have depicting a man and a woman connected by a beautiful copper heart. Every time I look at it, I am reminded that there is one Universal heart beating in us all—and each heart is precious.

2. When you bring your heart home, sit quietly and focus on it. Ask it to tell you about your own

heart. Ask it to remind you of what you have forgotten about your own love. Write down everything that it tells you. Ask it to remind you every day of the importance of your own heart and the hearts of all others. Put your heart in a place where you will see and remember every day how important it is. Like a glass of water that can be viewed as either half-full or half-empty, you can look at your heart and feel the love or feel the pain. The choice is yours.

Dr. Martin Luther King Jr. wrote a book entitled *Strength to Love*. It was a collection of sermons on the theme of love as a spiritual force that unites and strengthens all of life. As most are aware, Dr. King's life was dedicated to the spirit of unity and love. In 1967, he was delivering a lecture opposing war. He said, in part, "When I speak of love I am not speaking of some sentimental and weak response. I am speaking of that force which all of the great religions have seen as the supreme unifying principal of life. Love is the key that unlocks the door to ultimate reality."

Dr. King's words reflected his deep understanding that love must be extended to many. It is not enough to improve your own life. It is not enough to embrace only your immediate family and friends. Love must be practiced within the context of community, nation, and world. Love is a spiritual act that is committed to a way of behaving in everyday life that recognizes the interconnectedness of us all.

THE FLOWERS OF LOVE

Consider the love that resides within you as you might a flowering tree. The blooms are the flower of compassion, the flower of selfless giving, the flower of generosity, the flower of joy, and the flower of internal and external happiness. It is only when these flowers are in full bloom that we experience that which is love, and come to understand what it means to have Spirit move in us and through us. As we seek to uncover the sacred experience of love—daily—the love we attract into our lives is enhanced. The flowers that bloom in each person, that have their roots in the center of each heart, are the measures of the balance of the Universe. It is awesome to understand that the Universe is balanced (or not) based on our actions of love. In other words, each one of us is responsible for how the Universe will unfold. That is how powerful our love is.

Understanding that love is a natural quality of our being, and knowing that our humanness often separates us from our true nature, I invite you to become aware of the following flowers as a way of expanding the love that already exists within you. These flowers are not for use as leverage or barter material in relationships, nor are they something to brag about as superior accomplishments. These flowers are to assist you in connecting more deeply with your natural loving self and becoming a catalyst for all of life's spiritual awakening.

The Flower of Compassion

This flower blooms when we live openhearted in the moment, with our thoughts extending to others rather than focusing solely on ourselves. It is essential to understand that compassion is not a single act of kindness for another. Compassion is a way of life; it is how we are with ourselves and others in our daily life. It is an internal consciousness that continuously pays attention and responds to the needs of our bodies, minds, and spirits, while being sympathetic to the needs of others.

Compassion creates a softening around the edges of our heart that allows grace to flow through our lives and through the etheric body (energy field) of another who is in our presence. This reminds us that there is no separation between us. Compassion is not something we do, but something we are. Faithfully, we must demonstrate compassion, with ourselves and others, and trust the compassionate Universe to have it gracefully returned. Too often, before we are willing to give to others, we require them to prove that they are willing to give to us. Faith is doing it in the opposite order. "Give and you shall receive."

Gregg Braden, author of *Walking Between the Worlds: The Science of Compassion*, says, "Compassion is the kernel of your nature." In other words, compassion is natural.

Part of what keeps us from compassion is judgment. Judgment throws us off balance from the truth about ourselves and others. Judgment is not connected to the heart, and that which is not connected to the heart significantly reduces connection to humankind. Our ability to embrace all of our experiences—without judgment—is the key to compassion.

Having compassion does not imply having no boundaries. There is a fine line between displaying discernment and executing judgment. Discernment is an awareness that someone or something does not exist for our highest good, and therefore we act accordingly, guided by our intuition.

Judgment is drawing a conclusion about someone or something, usually based on a current or past fear.

Acting with compassion is the natural impulse of love that guides us through our daily lives. It offers us the opportunity to view and respond to ourselves and others from an enlightened state of being.

INNER EXPLORATION

1. Bring to mind and write down the most recent experience you have had with someone who invoked in you anger, fear, rage, or a desire for revenge. Notice the current of energy within you as you think about this person (or experience). That current is a live wire that is burning the vital energy of your life force. Our goal is to put out the fire.

2. Ask yourself, "Is there any way I can understand the pain in this other person that caused him or her to respond to me in this way?" Write down your response.

3. Write down the last experience you can remember in which you said or did something to someone that you still feel bad about. That current of energy is also a live wire that is burning the vital energy of your life force. Is there any way you can understand the pain in yourself that caused

you to respond to that particular person in a hurtful way?

4. Write a letter of compassion to the person by whom you felt hurt. Let the words come from your heart rather than your mind. Explain that you are choosing to see beyond the right or wrong of their action, and are choosing to bless them for bringing forth an opportunity for you to open more fully to compassion.

5. Write a letter of compassion to yourself, saying (and deeply meaning it) that you are choosing not to judge your actions as right or wrong. Recognize that you were in pain or in fear when you chose your response. You are now embracing your humanity, and are choosing to be compassionate with your shortcomings.

In writing the two letters, notice again that there is no separation between you and the other person. An act of compassion brings both your actions and the actions of others into balance and allows you to open yourself to love.

~~~~~~

The Flower of Selfless Giving

This flower blooms when we no longer need to wait to give to others until *after* we have come to understand them. Selfless giving occurs when we have faith in our own guidance, and can give of ourselves despite not knowing the entirety of another person or experience. Selfless giving, often called unconditional love, is a loving expression born of the soul that knows human understanding is not necessary for its expression. True self-worth and self-love are born during our acts of selfless giving. It is in not interpreting or analyzing what we feel moved to give that we find our holiness.

The logical mind needs to understand and feel safe before it allows us to give. We are wise to bypass that logical approach because it is the uncertainty, the *not* knowing why we are doing a particular thing, and the reliance on our intuition that moves us ever closer to faith and trust. In this mode, we allow ourselves a particular experience without wrapping our minds around the outcome, even when that experience seems difficult.

Several years ago I was going through what some call "the dark night of the soul." The night lasted for more than a year. I walked away from my business, I sank into a deep depression, and I had many thoughts of leaving Mother Earth. I went into my house, closed the door, and shut out life. I got very quiet.

Somewhere in the fourth or fifth month of this darkness, because I couldn't seem to do anything for myself, I felt a need to do something worthwhile for someone else.

I had been hearing a great deal on television about a school for homeless children that had recently opened up in Arizona. Good Morning America did a story on this school, calling it a model for the entire country. I knew that there were literally hundreds of people in line for volunteer positions. It came to me that I wanted to start a self-worth and self-esteem class for young girls at that school. I found it interesting that in the midst of my darkness—not having a clue where my own self-worth was lurking, and with no money coming in—I wanted to teach others about self-worth and self-esteem, for free. My inner guidance knew that the way out of my darkness was to give to others what I most needed.

Since my previous philanthropic endeavors had involved the homeless and families in crisis, I knew my past work would serve my present desire to help. Repeatedly, I called the school for an appointment with the human resource director. After two months of getting no response, I gathered up a modicum of strength and went over to the school. As soon as I walked through the doors, every color around me became vibrant, for the first time in months. I paused for a moment, feeling a shift within me. A light went on. The strength that I had always known so well seemed to be returning, welcoming me home. Without an appointment, I sauntered into the director's office. Resume in hand, I asked for her time—right then and there. Within an hour, I met with her, the school principal, and one of the school's psychologists. I convinced them that this program was necessary and I expressed my desire to begin immediately.

When I walked out of the school one hour later, perhaps I should have been surprised that I had their solid support and that my start date was the following Monday, but I wasn't. When I got there the next Monday, perhaps I should have been surprised that they had given me my own classroom to do with as I wished, but I wasn't.

What did surprise me was the lifting of my darkness as I taught those children what I myself needed to remember. I was also surprised a few months later when the school principal called me at home to have one of the most serious conversations I have ever had. She asked me to please come to the school immediately and attempt to break up a suicide pact. These children, she said, trusted me. She felt my influence and love would have a strong impact on their decision regarding their lives. I was stunned as I returned to the school. My own desire to leave Mother Earth suddenly departed. The knowledge that my life had deep meaning came home to me.

When I got to the school, the two girls were huddled together in the corner of the sofa I had bought to create a feeling of a living room in our classroom. For the next two and a half hours, I entered their model of the world. We discussed the value of their lives—and of all life. They told me about the pain and lovelessness of their childhood and family experience. So they could feel safe and not judged, I told them about my childhood, which wasn't that different from theirs.

I then led them lovingly out of that particular storm. They agreed to try life again.

The blessing continues, all these years later. While writing this story, I feel an overwhelming sense of love for myself, the staff, and the children who gave me the opportunity to have that teaching experience and to heal myself in the process.

Selfless giving is a wonderful way of outpouring love. What you give is always returned. The additional gift is in not needing to know in what form it will be returned or when.

Selfless giving is inspired by an ongoing conscious awareness of yourself and others. Opportunities for selfless giving spring up spontaneously when we live our lives creatively, generously, and lovingly.

INNER EXPLORATION

1. Reflect on selfless giving you could offer to the world. Notice what the energy of love within you invites you to do, and write it down. Selfless giving can be something as simple as holding a door open for a person on crutches, even if you are in a hurry, or committing to a project to help those less fortunate than you. It can be sending a card to someone because you have an instinct that this would be a good time to do that, or surprising your lover with a gift you know will delight them. Selfless giving can be buying a new outfit for a mother in a domestic shelter with whom you have no relationship, or inviting someone who is usually alone to dinner at your home. Follow through on the selfless giving you have chosen.

2. Selfless giving is balanced by giving to yourself as well. Reflect on what you might like to do for yourself. You could throw yourself a party even if it's not your birthday, or make an appointment for a healing-touch massage. Write down what you decide to give to yourself and follow through.

The Flower of Generosity

This bloom is the sister of selfless giving. The difference between them is slight. Generosity often carries with it a lightness, playfulness, or excitement that emerges from the spirit of the giver, instantaneously lifting the spirits of the receiver. When we watch a child's generosity, we can see their pure delight in the exchange and, if we watch closely, we will notice that once the experience is over, they go on with their life. They have no agenda; they don't wait for the big reaction. Their life does not depend on the receiver's response. Their generosity is simple and heartfelt.

Several years ago in the lobby of a family-in-crisis shelter where I did some work, I was waiting for one of the board members before a scheduled meeting. A mother and her eight-year-old daughter were also in the lobby. They had just been given the weekly award for the cleanest living quarters in the shelter. They were on their way to the shelter's storeroom, which was filled with donations of all kinds, to pick out a gift as their prize.

Holding her mommy's hand, the little girl gazed up and asked if they could please get a doll. The mother hugged her with great love and tenderness, and said, "I'm sorry, baby, but we need another blanket." The little girl didn't cry, didn't react, she only said, "Okay, Mommy." The pain in the mother's eyes at not being able to give her little girl a doll instead of the blanket was gut wrenching. The understanding of the child amazed me. After my meeting, I went out to a store and brought back a baby doll for the little girl. I gave it to her mother to give to her. The mother's eyes lit up as she thanked me and asked me my name; I asked hers and her daughter's. We then parted company.

When I came back the next week to teach a class, the mother and her daughter, Jessica, sought me out. Jessica gave me a page out of one of her coloring books. On the page were several angels outlined in black so they could be colored in. On the top of the page was the question, "Which angel is different from all the rest?" Jessica had colored in one of the angels and had written next to the question, "Maureen." After handing me the page, Jessica then went about her business in her natural, unpretentious, loving way. This time it was my eyes that lit up.

Generously given gifts are unexpected treasures, large or small, that we bestow upon another with all our heart, bringing instantaneous joy to both parties.

Being generous with "stuff," giving things unexpectedly to friends and strangers alike, has always been part of my nature. People's joy in receiving always brought joy to me.

At one point in my life, a friend suggested that I gave to people in order to gain their acceptance. I was moved to look deep within myself to investigate that idea. This is what bubbled up: While giving things was very easy for me, I had trouble being generous with my heart. I let people get only so close to me, and then I would stop them. I was afraid that if they really knew all about me, they wouldn't find me lovable. I was ashamed of my childhood and ashamed of my behavior and the choices I had made as a result of a dysfunctional childhood. I recalled my ex-husband telling me that there was a part of me he would never know. I actually thought that was a good thing! I was unaware that I was not generous in the giving of *all* of myself. Unable to give of myself completely, my giving of "things" was my way of avoiding that issue, and it tricked me into believing that I was a generous person.

I discovered that the complete meaning of generosity could not be found in the giving of things alone, but in giving all of me to those who have chosen me, or whom I have chosen to share in my life. In becoming generous with all aspects of myself—my attention, my concern, my love—coupled with my joy in giving to others, I discovered the true nature of generosity.

INNER EXPLORATION

Here is another opportunity to write about yourself from the truth of your heart, not the thoughts in your mind.

1. What is given selflessly will always come back to you at the appropriate moments in your life. Ask yourself the following questions. Where in your life can you give more generously in order to fill a part of you that seems empty and in need? Do you need more joy? More love? More time? More patience? Is your need financial? Do you desire to be a better friend, a better listener, more spontaneous or lighthearted? Whatever you feel you need is the very thing you need to give more generously. If you feel fearful in giving the very thing you feel you need, remember that fear is an acronym for False Evidence Appearing Real. If fear remains in command of your actions, you will continue to linger in a life of not receiving what you need most.

2. Give something spontaneously five times in the next week to an unsuspecting recipient. You can give a generous smile or a generous donation. Whatever you do, have fun with your generosity! And then keep on giving more.

Where someone else may choose to be less generous and more fearful, your generosity and light-heartedness will greatly assist in establishing the loving balance of Mother Earth and all her children.

The Flower of Joy

This flower blooms fully when we choose our pathways in life in direct correlation to our hearts. Joy grins from ear to ear and from the inside out, simply carrying itself with the self-assurance that all is well, right here and now, in this moment. Joy can only be obtained by returning to our true state of being—pure love—and letting go of the need for obstacles in life to provide us with stimulation.

Joy is our natural state, and our challenge is to stop empowering any belief systems that separate us from it. When we make our decisions from a place of sacredness not scared-ness, we simplify the experience of life and reencounter joy. In the book *Life Without Conditions*, author and channel Glenda Green quotes Jesus as saying, "If we surround our sacred experiences with endless requirements sanctioned by man, then basically we have shut the doors to Heaven."

Joy comes from the soul through the hallway of the heart that leads to the mind. If you are enduring your life devoid of joy, it is a sign that you are directing your thoughts inappropriately, and you are off track. The invitation of life is to experience love and joy by connecting with the wisdom and simplicity of the heart and soul, rather than be misled by the mind and its shouting orders. It's our job to guard our thoughts and direct them as the information travels from the soul to the heart and into the mind, instead of letting them direct us.

Joy is an energy that is sustained by directed thinking, taking as many excursions as possible away from mental activity, and keeping an open heart. Carl Jung said, "If you are unhappy, you are too high up in your mind." When we sustain joy, there is nothing to do but have the experience of it and then give it away to others so they, too, can enjoy the experience. On the other hand, thought is a high-maintenance activity. It comes and goes, it changes positions, it interrupts and persuades, and it orders and disrupts. Our thoughts invariably cause complexities, while joy is simple. Still your thoughts and joy will dawn of its own accord.

What I noticed about my life some years ago was that I wasn't paying close enough attention to where my joy was coming from. I was so busy taking orders from my mind about what I was or wasn't supposed to do with my life, that I missed the obvious. I concocted all kinds of creative stories about how this would probably lead to that, and thought for hours on end about what I should do next. My mind took me the long way around the block and my joy was elusive.

Joy came in spurts and didn't last long. I was soon back to trying to figure out my life instead of listening to my life.

My joy always came when I was involved with teaching, speaking, or being a guest on a television or radio show. That was not my ego; that was my soul telling me that my work here on this planet was to give information to large groups of people. My joy came when I could be an instrument of loving information to assist others in finding their way, their peace. Believe it or not, it also came when I would arrive at the other side of a major life experience and "get it," that is, get what it meant, and then be able to share it with others. Those experiences enabled me to communicate to others that they were not alone and life hadn't singled them out for trials and tribulations.

Whatever you are resisting the most in your life right now is likely the very thing that will bring you the most joy. I resisted writing this book for six years. I told myself I didn't have enough time, I wouldn't be a good enough writer, and I wasn't smart enough to measure up to other authors I respected and admired. Not writing this book haunted me day and night until the only thing I could do to get rid of the pressure was to write it, regardless of the outcome. Need I tell you the joy that writing this book is giving me? And at this moment, I have no idea of the outcome. What I do know is that my soul, my heart, and my mind are filled with joy and experiencing the proverbial field day!

INNER EXPLORATION

1. Think about and make a list of the moments in your life that have brought you joy. Such a moment could be when you were caring for animals or singing in the choir, the shower, or the car. Perhaps it was when you helped elderly people or children in need. Maybe it's when you are immersed in your physical fitness or out playing in nature; playing a musical instrument; preparing food or preparing a seminar. It may well be when you are writing or painting into the wee hours of the night.

2. In your list of experiences, you will find a common thread. For example, you may notice that you have always loved writing. Perhaps as a child you wrote stories, as an adult you wrote magazine articles or poems, and you've always kept a journal. Follow that or any thread. That's the clue to finding your joy. Go for it!

Don't let anyone's judgment, particularly your own, get in the way of your joy, your love. Mother Teresa said, "Joy is prayer. Joy is strength. Joy is love. Joy is a net by which you can catch souls."

The Flower of Internal and External Happiness

This flower opens when the flowers of compassion, selfless giving, generosity, and joy are in full bloom. Each of the flowers has its roots inside you. How they show themselves outwardly will depend on how you maintain them inwardly. Internal and external happiness arises from your tending of these flowers. Internal and external happiness is fertile soil for love. When we fully understand love, we are unable to see it as something outside ourselves and we know that even the most adverse conditions of life can in no way undermine it.

There is only one aspect of life that you need ever be devoted to: Love. *Timeless Wisdom* quotes writer Og Mandino as saying, "Beginning today, treat everyone you meet as if they were going to be dead by midnight. Extend to them all the care, kindness, and understanding you can muster, and do so with no thought of any reward. Your life will never be the same."

If you were on your deathbed, would there be one single thing more important to you in your final moments than being loved or having loved well? I think not.

Love, the second aspect of BLISS, reveals the meaning of life. By becoming one with love, we become one with life.

CHAPTER 3

*I*ntegrity

A double-minded man is unstable in all of his ways.

—James 1:8

When the acronym BLISS—Balance, Love, Integrity, Sexuality, and Soul—came to me, it was clear that the "I" represented **Integrity**. While considering the unfolding of this chapter, it also became clear to me that Integrity is always backed with **Intention,** and so I have woven the two together to represent the "I" in BLISS.

Integrity exists when our intention (thought) is focused and held on that which is positive, loving, kind, and righteous.

Integrity does not exist without thoughtful feelings, backed by the power source of emotions, loving words, and creative action that seek a positive outcome for all involved. Love backs integrity. Simply put, integrity backed with intention means that what we think, feel, say, and do are all in consistent loving harmony with one another.

Intention, on the other hand, can exist without integrity. A good example of intention without integrity is actions of violence and destruction, or consciously made decisions that in some way harm another emotionally or physically. That is intention backed with fear.

When we are in integrity, our thoughts, feelings, emotions, words, and deeds are in harmony and we bring balance into our inner and outer worlds. (Note that feeling and emotion are not the same. Emotion plus thought equals feeling. For example, if you're repeatedly told as a child that you're not good enough, you will store emotions such as grief or anger. These emotions then fuel negative thoughts that lead to feelings of worthlessness, shame, unlovability, etc. Emotions—for example, love—can also lead to positive thoughts and feelings. In fueling our thoughts, emotion is a tremendous source of power.)

For Mahatma Gandhi, having integrity was the definition of happiness. My belief is that acting with integrity creates feelings of happiness and well-being. Many of us think one thing, say another, then do something else somewhere in between. Why? Because of our fear of being rejected by other people and society in general, or because we don't trust ourselves.

Since integrity is not fully understood, we collectively lack a large piece of the magical universal pie. Most people believe that integrity means being honest in our dealings with others, particularly in business. While that is not wholly incorrect, it is not wholly accurate either. Something is missing in our understanding, and we can't incorporate that which we don't fully understand. Integrity does indeed encompass honesty in our dealings with others. What many people have not embraced, however, is that integrity also encompasses honesty within ourselves, where no one else is involved. The commonly held definition of integrity is like a half-finished sentence—we can't derive total meaning from something incomplete.

Ralph Waldo Emerson wrote, "Nothing is at last sacred but the integrity of your own mind."

Many years ago, I was teaching a series of one-hour classes on self-worth and self-esteem to families in crisis at a shelter in Mesa, Arizona. (By now, I'm sure you realize that my commitment to working with those who don't have access to books, seminars, and retreats is very important to me.) I never seem to prepare conventionally to teach a class. I always have a topic in mind, but rather enjoy hearing what I might have to say if I don't etch everything in stone beforehand. For one class, the topic of the day was the importance of being happy and not having to be right all the time. What it became was a class about integrity.

I felt rather "out of body" during the class and observed myself as I spoke. After completing the hour, and spending another forty-five minutes answering questions, I got into my car for the long drive home. In reflecting on my words and the responses from the people in the class, I felt chills running though me. I realized at that moment that I had just taught a class, again, about something that I myself needed to incorporate—integrity, integrity within myself. I became aware of the numerous times that what I felt, what I said, and what I did were not in harmony. I was aware that there were times when I was feeling one thing but said something else; and other times, I would do something that didn't represent my feelings.

Throughout the drive home, I asked myself why. The answers that came to me were that I didn't trust myself and didn't feel that the real me would be acceptable to others. There were times when I believed that someone would leave me if I spoke my truth from my heart. So, like a chameleon, I would shift and change to accommodate my surroundings and those in it. It saddened me to realize that I would betray myself to win acceptance from others. And I asked myself, "Are you really doing people a favor by acting in a misleading way?"

By the time I got home, I knew I had more work to do within myself. I would not teach another class about integrity until I could walk the talk. I began immediately to do my best to exemplify all that I had taught about integrity. At times, it was a painful, laborious process as part of what had become normal behavior died off. Ultimately, it was a beautiful and exhilarating process. We receive so much when we just allow ourselves to be and express Who We Really Are.

THE PATH TO INTEGRITY

Gaining integrity requires first and foremost an honest, non-ego-centered evaluation of who you are and how you live your life. That needs to be followed by an intense desire to be different from what you are right now. You must establish the intention that you are willing to be your complete, congruent, authentic self and send that intention out into the Universe with passionate devotion to its realization. Then you must match your actions to your intention. If the outer you tells the Universe one thing, and the inner you does not believe you are capable of change or is unwilling to go through what it takes to change, you will immediately polarize your objective.

The old adage "The road to hell is paved with good intentions" comes from the familiar experience of forming an intention in the mind, but not wholly believing in it and then neglecting it or failing to follow through. In other words, we believe in the intention some of the time, but not enough of the time, and then we are mystified and angry that nothing has resulted except further confusion. That is the hell we create by not honoring our intentions. We must believe, think, feel, and accept as true the intention to become a person of integrity.

INTENTIONS

Thoreau wrote, "If one advances confidently in the direction of his dreams, and endeavors to live the life which he has imagined, he will meet with a success unexpected in common hours." Intentions are unfailingly the magnet of the Universe. They must accompany us wherever we go as though they are attached to our very breath.

Every intention possesses within it the means for fulfillment. Through our intentions we can literally create something out of nothing. In other words, we have the power to fulfill our own dreams and desires, which spares us from expecting someone else to do it for us. We can enjoy our personal relationships without expectations, which comes as a great relief to everyone.

Intentions must be very specific. If you were to say to the Universe (or God), "I intend to change my behavior," or "I don't want to be without integrity any more," or even, "I want to own my own company," the Universe is receiving a very abbreviated request. You must be much more specific.

When I tackled the issue of integrity, I wrote in my journal, "Dear God, I have spent my life in distrust of myself and others. I am aware that I have betrayed myself in the following areas:..."

(I then listed as many areas of betrayal as I could remember.) I continued, "I am aware that I have cheated myself and others by not saying what I was feeling at the time and also by blocking the feelings that I was really having. I am aware that I often feel one thing, but say another in order to make someone feel better at my expense, or at times to make someone feel bad so I can feel better. I am also aware that I make commitments to do certain things and when the time comes to do them, I regret having made the commitment because I really didn't want to do that to begin with. My intention is to become a person of integrity, and I am willing to do whatever it takes to make that happen. Please, dear God, help me, and I will do my part in being conscious of my feelings, my words, and my actions. Thank you very much."

It is important to understand that once you have made your intentions clear to the Universe—whether it is to become a person of integrity, CEO of a company, owner of a car dealership, a great mother, or terrific friend—you must be prepared for the manner in which the Universe responds to your request. What I know to be true is this: When I consciously decided to become a person of integrity, with rapid fire the experiences that I attracted (or the Universe sent to me) put me in a position to slip easily back into my old behavior of thinking one thing, saying another, and doing something in between. I couldn't believe how many times I was willing to compromise myself because at the time it was easier to betray myself than to be true to myself.

DETACHING FROM THE OUTCOME

With our clear and heartfelt intentions sent off on the wings of an angel, we must detach ourselves from how we think the response will appear, and be prepared to be tested. Once we do our part in creating and sending out our intentions, the receiver, God, the Great Universal Energy, will respond in due time. Our job then is to be conscious of and work toward being integrated within, that is, becoming a person of integrity. In order to bring forth a new aspect of ourselves, we must assume that the potential is already within us, and we must be willing to eliminate the fear that causes non-integrated behavior. Watch yourself, and be as interested in what goes on inside of you—when you are in conflict in what you feel, say, and do—as you are in what happens outside you.

When you send your intention to the Universe, you must have faith that the Universe will receive and answer it. If you mailed a letter from Detroit to Canada, you wouldn't run to the air carrier or the post office to make sure it arrived. You know and trust that the postal service will handle mail going to a specific person at a specific place you can't see. You must apply the same faith here. Your intention will reach its destination and be answered. First, set the intention, then detach from the outcome while simultaneously holding an unwavering faith that the intention will be made manifest, co-created by the Universe and your commitment.

Between setting an intention and the manifestation of it, we always go through a process. It's like a road trip. If you drive from New York to Florida, you pass through many states in order to arrive at your destination. It's the same with intentions—you pass through many different stages of self-evolvement or states between envisioning an intention and realizing it. In each state of the New York–Florida trip, you encounter different weather—sometimes thunderous rains and snow, other times sunshine and clear skies. The weather changes; it always does. Your stages of evolvement will change, too, as your journey progresses. When you reach your destination, endowed with greater strength, your fully manifested intention will be there waiting for you.

INNER EXPLORATION

1. Before beginning, find your silence within. Once you are still, look at your life, all parts of your life—personal and professional, internal and external. Ask yourself, "Am I living a life of complete integrity?"

2. If your answer is "yes," God bless you! If your answer is "some of the time" or "not really," write down the areas where you are not acting with integrity, keeping in mind the full definition of integrity as you respond.

3. Answer the following questions and add any others that come to mind.

    (a) Do I resent my job?

    (b) Do I resent my present relationship?

    (c) Do I resent my children?

    (d) Am I carrying any unresolved resentment toward anyone in my life right now?

(e) Do I feel as though I am being taken advantage of?

(f) Do I feel that I have missed out on any part of the dream I had for my life? If so, who am I blaming?

4. Now it's time to take responsibility for each area of concern that you listed. Write down what you need to do differently, beginning right now, to start living your life with integrity. Your list can include simple things, such as making a life-changing decision never to argue with your mother again, or more involved choices, such as sitting down with a friend and having a heart-to-heart talk about the truth of what you are really feeling.

Recreating situations past or present doesn't necessarily have to involve anyone but you. Just begin the process—unwaveringly, compassionately, and lovingly—and if you stay within your heart as you make your decisions, you will know what to do.

FOLLOW THE DOTS

When people ask me how I live my life, I tell them I follow the dots. "What does that mean?" they often ask. My response is as follows: When we have faith in the Universe, we know there are a number of energies involved in the playing out of our lives. Although we can't see all the players, I believe they send telepathic messages that I can receive through my intuition. Then I can act on the messages or not. I call that following the dots. I believe that when we follow the dots, we are led to great treasures.

This is one of my follow-the-dots stories.

Years ago I had just returned home to Arizona from one of my many summer vacations in Laguna Beach, California. As I was unpacking my suitcase, I clearly received guidance (or heard my intuition) saying that I should return to Laguna Beach. My first reaction was that I must be making this up, that I just wanted to go back because I love it there. Understanding the importance of listening to guidance, however, whether or not it appears foolish to the outside world, I repacked my suitcase a week later and went back to California.

Once there, I called a new friend I had just met a couple of weeks earlier and announced to her that I was guided to come back, but didn't know why. She said, "Maureen, I know why you're back. Just after you left, I met a very interesting and wise man, and I felt strongly that you were to meet him. He is a man with great spiritual insight and I believe he has a message for you." That evening she arranged for me to meet this man.

Entering his modest home, I felt a loving energy surround me. His eyes reminded me of the blue-green cat's-eye marbles I had played with as a child. It seemed as though he didn't look at me; instead, he seemed to look through me into the depths of my soul.

"What are you looking for?" he asked.

"I am looking for peace, deep inner peace, and I am also looking for the joy that I know is the partner of that peace," I answered.

"What are you willing to give up for this?"

"Whatever it takes," I replied.

The man studied me for what seemed like an eternity before he spoke again. "It takes great courage to seek oneself. Through your intention, created from love for yourself, your soul will create and bring you experiences so that your wish for inner peace is made manifest. Your particular intention will bring about great change in all aspects of your life. Know that you have already been given everything you need to handle these changes. You may not like every experience you have, and it may not occur in the manner that you think it should; however, know that once your intention is released to the Universe, you will receive loving guidance and assistance from the nonphysical realm, every step of the way. The moment you wholeheartedly create your intention, the Universe in all its benevolence rallies to support you. You must still your mind and open your heart to draw upon the wisdom and compassion that will be given to you from the unseen."

We talked long into the night, and I came home two days later.

Most of us spend a lifetime setting intentions in motion. The vast majority of the time, our intentions are unconscious. But every intention we create, consciously or unconsciously, sets energy into motion. When we establish an intention based on negatives—fear, need, lack, greed, or revenge—we create imbalance, or negative karma. Simply put, karma is any action we take—in thought, word, or deed—and its response, which inevitably comes back to us. Rephrased in today's wisdom, a definition of karmic balance is "What goes around, comes around." That is why the intention behind the original thought, word, and deed is so crucially important. Karma is Universal Law, unimpeachable, unable to be put aside, inescapable. Please do not take lightly that "whatsoever you sow, so shall you reap." Karma is a universal and impersonal mandate. Everything that is happening to you right now and has happened to you in the past is a result of the way you make or have made choices or created intentions. Everything!

When we set forth an incomplete intention, one not fully formed, we create imbalance. The moment we set forth a clear, complete, conscious intention, designed with love for the highest good of all concerned, we will begin to find balance. Good, honest intentions, forged with the iron of integrity, come from a clear, thoughtful, loving mind.

THE MIND AS HYPNOTIST

In order to harmonize our emotions, feelings, words, and deeds, we must learn to use our minds differently from the way we have become accustomed to using them. Our assignment is to retrain the mind away from its "normal" way of thinking back to its natural way. Our goal is to break free from the mind of man, which is limited, to inhabit the Mind of God, which is unlimited and illuminated. The normal way in which we use the mind is what we *see*, we believe. In truth, what we *believe* is what we see. What we see depends not so much on what is actually there as on the assumptions we make when we look. Those assumptions are based on our personal belief systems and automatic judging systems.

We have had a very intimate, long-standing relationship with our minds. It is primarily the mind that has given us our definitions of ourselves and others. The mind has been everything to us from our own "Dear Abby" to our personal visionary. We have relied on it, expected it to perform for us, and taken for granted that it will always do its best for us. We have been misled by the mind's self-importance, however. Our minds do not show us the way to enlightenment. Instead, the mind fills us with expectations, insistence, and interpretations and, through its self-protective instincts, does not allow for the pure potential that emanates from the free-flowing energy of the Universe.

We are also limited by ego, a part of the mind that makes judgments based on a limited perspective. The ego keeps us from making progress by anchoring us to the "I" of who we think we are. The ego doesn't encourage the contemplation of change. It clings to its own concept of who we are and what we need: I know who I am, I can't help it, I just think this way; I know I'm right; I hate this, I love that; I have to have this in order to be happy. The ego is needy and has a voracious appetite, demanding constant feeding.

To move beyond these limitations, it is necessary to still the mind long enough to become aware of the difference between mind, ego, and higher wisdom, and realize which one has the greatest integrity and is the most honest.

Do you really trust your mind to the extent that you would trust it with your life? When you really think about it, what has it actually proven to you, what has it given to you? The mind was designed to solve problems of logic, as in science and mathematics, and to answer questions such as whether you'll need a heavy coat on a trip to Alaska or whether you should eat, since you haven't had a meal all day. But the mind was never designed to solve the larger problems of life. In *Life Without Conditions*, Glenda Green cites

Jesus as saying, "The mind has no power to change your life. That privilege belongs to the heart."

When you have gone through moments of despair because of childhood woes or dismantled love affairs, you have most likely *analyzed* the situation. Has your mind ever solved the dilemma for you? Did it ever even disagree with you about your perception of the events? Did it give you the answers you wanted to hear, or teach you something new about yourself? How often did it take you on a long ride through the back alleys of accusation, guilt, shame, blame, and judgment?

One of my spiritual teachers compared the human mind to a hypnotist. She asked me if I had ever seen a hypnotist perform at a dinner theater or on television. She described a scene with me onstage with a hypnotist, who put me in a trance and said, "For the next half hour, I want you to do exactly what I tell you. Perhaps I will tell you to bark like a dog, maybe I'll have you walk around like a penguin, or perhaps I'll have you pretend to climb a ladder, and then I'll have you act as if you are eating a hamburger. When I snap my fingers, you will come out of the trance." The mind is no different from a hypnotist. When you ask the mind for answers to life's questions, it makes up a story and we follow it as if we were in a trance.

If you went to your mind for advice about your ex-husband and your past perceptions of him were negative, the mind would back up your negative thoughts. It would no doubt give you something like this: "The guy is a loser. He's emotionally unavailable and a selfish jerk. He was a complete waste of time. There's probably another woman I don't know about. He doesn't even know what love is." Guided by your mind, you might respond with the thoughts, "I'm glad to be out of that relationship. He wasn't my type anyway. He's got a big ego and I can't stand his friends." Before you know it, hours, days, weeks, months, or even years go by, and you've received nothing from your mind but rhetoric. It has solved none of your life's concerns.

Our mind chatter literally hypnotizes us. It takes up eons of our precious time to no end and with no value. And it isn't only over the larger issues of life that the mind puts us into a trance; it happens with the little day-to-day concerns, too. Here's a great example of the mind leading me around by my nose until I realized what was happening and broke the trance.

I went to my hairdresser for a haircut. I had always believed that I had inherited from my father a compulsion about how perfect my hair needed to look. My hairdresser always spent a ridiculous amount of time cutting my hair. There were times I would have to say, "Mark, I need to go to work today!" I would take two hours out of my day to get a haircut, but I went to him because he was an absolute perfectionist who gave me the absolutely perfect haircut.

One day after one of these two-hour haircuts, I realized that he had cut my hair far too short. When I climbed into my car, the big problem solver in my life (my mind) kicked in. "What a lousy haircut! I can't believe how short my hair is. I have a big event to go to next Friday and my hair is still going to look horrible. I'm going to look terrible! This haircut makes me look old. Maybe I should go to the tanning booth and get a tan, then my hair won't look so short and I'll look better. Damn Mark! He's such a pain in the ass to deal with. I can't believe how much time he takes to cut my hair and then he blow-dries it for so long, no wonder it looks dry. I'm sick of him taking up so much of my time!"

This was my conversation for forty minutes straight while I was looking in my car mirror every three minutes to see how my hair looked. *I was literally in a trance until I realized what I was doing and snapped out of it—for a while.*

A few days later, I went to dinner at a friend's house, and she said, "Did you get your hair cut?" Oh, perfect, thought my mind, another opportunity to put Maureen into a trance. I fell into the trance quickly, " Yes, I got my hair cut and it looks terrible and I'm so damn mad at Mark, blah…blah…blah…!" And there we were, my mind and I, off and running again. We ran until I became exhausted with it and simply stopped.

Do you see what the mind does? It distorts and takes us on a crazy journey to the middle of nowhere, solving absolutely nothing, while we follow it as if in a trance. We literally *make up our minds* about everything. That is why integrity is often elusive. The mind is saying one thing, our feelings are saying something else, and we're doing something in between. We have let the mind take the lead and we have come to rely upon a made-up interpretation of life. If what the mind makes up is true, how do you explain three people seeing the same movie with one person thinking it was great, a second thinking it was okay, while the third walked out because it was so bad? Who is right? They all are, even though there are three different opinions and three distinct perspectives. There is no absolute truth about life that can be evidenced through our thoughts.

What we as humans don't tap into as readily is the Mind of God, the Universal Mind, which is as available to us as the next bus coming along. This is where the gold is, where life's answers lie, where Universal Truth resides, and it allows us to access the latent power that is within all of us. There is no power source for life's problems in the human mind. That is not to say that the mind is not important. It *is* to say that the mind is greatly enhanced when we quiet it down, eradicate its base of fear, and balance it with the higher wisdom of the Universal Mind, the Mind of God.

So how do we learn to connect with the Mind of God and, in balance with the mind of man, gain and retain integrity? We suit up and go into inner space.

BEING MEDITATION

Several years ago, I was walking on a beach in California. I had just finished reading a book that had deeply touched me. As I walked on the warm sand, feeling the heat of the sun on my back and listening to the songs of the seabirds, I felt at one with everything around me and within me. There wasn't a thought in my head—I was in a moving state of meditation. I had a deep feeling of gratitude for the author who had written the book, for my ability to understand the meaning layered between the words, for being able to be on this beach at this particular time, and for just being alive at that moment. As I finished my walk and returned to where my towel lay on the sand, I was aware of a peaceful smile on my face that felt comfortably at home.

It was almost dinnertime and I decided to go back to the hotel and have dinner at my favorite restaurant. Feeling peaceful by myself and not wanting to have a conversation with anyone, I decided to dine alone. I went down to the restaurant and asked for my favorite table, which gave me a panoramic view of the ocean, the mountains, and the sun that was about to set. I could also see a patch of lawn leading down to the boardwalk where people of diverse ethnic backgrounds were walking, sitting on benches, or playing Frisbee with their dogs. I realized I still had that same smile on my face from hours before; others in the dining room seemed to notice, too, as their eyes met mine and they smiled.

*Just after ordering my dinner, something happened to me that
I had never experienced before.*

*A feeling of immense love washed over me. In a matter of
moments, I didn't know where the waves of the ocean ended and
I began. I became the beauty of the setting sun and the strength of
the mountains. I was the heartbeat of every person walking on
the lawn and the joy of every dog catching a Frisbee. I was each
blade of grass and every soaring bird. I was everywhere and I
was everything. Tears began to roll down my cheeks, and I didn't
brush them away. Sitting there at the table in what I now know
was a state of bliss, I knew what it felt like to know God—to be at
one with everything, to be everything.*

*When I became aware of myself, more than an hour had
passed. My food remained untouched and, amazingly, no one in
the restaurant had approached me. As if on cue, my waiter came
over and simply asked if I would like a cup of tea. With tears still
glistening on my cheeks, I looked up at him with immense love
and simply said "yes." This was the deepest meditation I had ever
entered, and inside that deep inner silence I knew the truth of who
I was. The recognition of who I really was, no longer limited or
separate from All That Is, ended my preoccupied cycle of self-
involvement, and began the true journey of self-discovery, which
knows no limits. I felt as though I had just been born into this
world.*

*Later that evening, I realized that my practice of meditating
had led me to a place where I didn't have to go into meditation. I
was meditation itself in the stillness of my thoughts and in the
balance of my emotions and feelings. This was the manifestation
of integrity: Everything inside and outside of me was lovingly at
one. The inner experience changed my outer life forever; it
changed the concept of who I was, and who and what everything
was around me. This is not to say that I didn't (or don't now) slip
back into old patterns of thought once in a while. But that expe-*

*rience at the beach gave me a memory I could always come home
to. It gave me a truth to replace every lie I had ever been told or
told myself about who I was and who everyone else was. God
knew my pure intention to know myself and gave me a tour behind the veils of separation. My false, suffering self collapsed long
enough for me to experience my true nature—the nature of bliss.
As long as I live on this earth, I can never again fear or pretend
that I don't know Who I Am and that I am not connected to everyone and everything.*

THE MEDITATION JOURNEY

Meditation or stillness doesn't always take us on a journey like this. It takes us on different journeys in different ways
at different times. The goal of meditation is to quiet the mind
so we can experience who we are, expand our consciousness,
and establish a balance between our inner and outer worlds.
When we deepen our natural state of relaxation, enabling us
to see the truth of who we are and experience love on every
level of our being, meditation can lead to what we call su-
pernormal powers.

The retraining of the mind in meditation requires a
single-pointed attention. We have all experienced single-
pointed attention in our lives; it happens when we are doing something we truly love, whether it's cooking a wonderful meal, making love, or playing a game of tennis. In daily
life, our single-pointed attention typically splinters into several simultaneous thoughts, which leads us to try to do one
thing while thinking about another. Look how well we have
mastered driving a car while talking on a cell phone! This
multitasking mastery will not lead us to enlightenment.

When we learn, during meditation, the power of single-pointed attention, and we witness what meditation can accomplish, we will soon be able to extend this same single-pointed attention into our daily lives in order to extract the full potential from each experience.

The mind is not accustomed to *us* leading *it*. It has had us on a leash for years! In the practice of meditation, we begin to guide the mind back to its natural state, which is to co-create with God, whose only request is for us to keep part of our mind open so His/Her guidance can enter and reveal the highest, most enlightened view. Instead of analyzing the events of the day before us or behind us, as we usually do, we can sequester ourselves in a quiet place and travel inward to that precious space where greater truths can visit and be made welcome. Relieved of its normal duties, giving us a much-needed reprieve, the mind emerges in a state of exalted calm, which Deepak Chopra calls "pure potential."

In its simplest form, meditation renews our energy while allowing us to gather together all the separate parts of ourselves that have been scattered about. Meditation is a place where we meet with God and our guides and teachers of the Light. It is where we listen instead of talk. The constant motion and chatter of our lives leave little room for those of the Light to get a word in edgewise. There must be a pause in which the voice of God or any of our guides can be heard. The ancients have written, "Space is the Great Mother of Life." One must create space by emptying one's mind in order to hear love, extract wisdom, and give birth to creativity.

Meditation has been handed down to us as a gift from wise sages and saints who lived thousands of years ago. They knew that meditation was the key to self-understanding and would create balance between the voices of the outer world—fueled by ego, agenda, and fear—and the voices of the inner world, warmed by love and compassion. Eastern teachings often speak of meditation as "the way to inner integrity."

For thousands of years, it has been a custom in the Eastern world to turn inward in silence to find God and to know oneself as the image and likeness of the Great Divine. By contrast, it has been common practice in Western culture to find ourselves in a building with an authority figure standing in the pulpit telling us about God. When we leave the building, we have no knowledge of our own divinity or *our* truth about God. We have forgotten that God is within us. There is no place outside yourself where you will find your wholeness, your holiness. It's not enough for me to tell you this, or to try to convince you that it's true. Personal stories about being one with God, experiencing our true nature, and dancing with bliss are also not enough. You are personally invited to experience the value of meditation (or stillness, if you prefer).

Meditation stabilizes the heart and mind and allows that special space of pure intention to be made manifest. When our minds and hearts are stabilized by stillness, there is a powerful shift in consciousness that enables clarity to create an expanded and refined awareness of Self.

When you turn inward, you will experience for yourself the shift that is inevitable. With that shift, you will welcome the balanced ebb and flow of an experience, rather than hanging on tightly and trying to control it. You will be aware of the intensification of an experience and then its dissolving into nothingness, leaving behind a trailing wake of self-discovery. In the privacy of your inner space, you will begin to have an intimate relationship with your true self, your soul, and God. In time, your inner space will merge with your outer space and create the balance that allows for the fulfillment of life "far from the madding crowd," where loud minds and even louder voices have no parking spaces. The inner and the outer merge to create bliss.

When we meditate, we become aware of the sacredness of our inner space, and once having been there, we yearn to return. *Knowledge* comes from the outside in; *wisdom* moves from the inside out. Many people ask me how I learned to hear God and how I came to know my guides. My answer is simply that I got quiet and I went within. With continued practice, I was able to hear their voices—even over the noisy chatter in a crowded restaurant.

Voices of Resistance

There are three common arguments people use to resist meditating. The first one is "My mind just won't stop, I can't meditate." That's the point about the mind. It tells you what's happening—"I can't meditate"—and you believe it. Have you checked in with yourself recently for an update on the truth of what you can or cannot do? Is your mind the ultimate decision-maker for you?

The second argument is "There's just not enough time in my day." Again, this is the voice of the ever-present, ever-insistent mind telling you what you do or do not have. Once again the mind has usurped your power and is leading you. Let me share this story with you about "enough time."

I had a very busy practice. There were days in the beginning stages of my company, BLISS, when I would be booked with clients from 9 a.m. until 7 p.m., Monday through Friday. My mind decided I needed to see as many clients as possible, so I could make as much money as possible to take care of all my wants and needs. Prior to starting BLISS, I practiced yoga three morn-

ings a week. *Yoga was one of my greatest joys and brought great balance to my life, even through rough days. My busy schedule, however, curtailed my yoga practice.*

One day I announced to my secretary that on Mondays, Wednesdays, and Fridays I would not be in until 11 a.m., as I was going to attend my favorite yoga class at 8:30 a.m. on those days. My secretary's concern was how I would see all of my clients with this new schedule. I knew it would all work out because I knew I could create my reality by my thoughts alone. I would not be trapped or victimized by the illusion of time. So I began my yoga classes again. I also decided to see fewer clients in order to create more balance in my life. My existing clients became accustomed to my schedule and many even took up the practice of yoga as they witnessed my refound joy in going back to class.

When I realized that I was about to begin writing this book, my first thought was, "Where will I find the time?" I announced to myself that I would make the time. Given that time, as we know it, is a man-made illusion to separate events and experiences on planet Earth, I could create my own time to accommodate writing, as well as take yoga classes and see my clients. I began by taking two days a week to write and three days to see clients. Again, everything worked out for the highest good of all concerned, just as I had intended. My clients accepted my changes because I accepted my changes. A little farther down the road, I completely changed the hours of my practice to accommodate my writing. This book had become of paramount importance to me.

We have come to accept time as though it were an immovable mountain. We use time as an excuse not to do that which serves our highest good. We become so overwhelmed and restrained by what we already do in the space of our time that we let time and our minds dictate our lives. Our days are so consumed by what we *think* we have to do, and how we *believe* we have to do it, that our souls get left out in the cold. We don't attend to the healing of our souls, the very reason we came to this planet—and we use time as an excuse. If you want to find time, look around you. It's everywhere. Make of it what you will; everything else will find its place.

The third and perhaps most reasonable and honest argument in resisting meditation is "I don't know how to meditate." That may be true, but if you wanted to learn to ski, wouldn't you make a point of finding an instructor?

Meditation may not always be an easy process, especially when you first begin. But neither is skiing. You begin on the bunny slope and advance with practice. In the process of learning, you fall frequently because you are unaccustomed to this new form of moving and lose control. In meditation, the mind is like the beginner trying to ski on icy snow: it slips and slides everywhere until we learn how to control it. Saint Teresa of Avila described the human mind as "an unbroken horse that would go anywhere except where you wanted it to."

The greatest argument in favor of meditation is that it demonstrates the existence of a distinctly different part of our nature that is typically not revealed during the first half of adult life. In the first half of life as adults, we understand our existence to be task oriented. We see life as a series of hurdles and obstacles that we must overcome in order to accomplish our goals. We concentrate on how to function in the outer world to the best of our ability, and we form an identity of who we think we are. Many of us reach a point of awakening, typically in our late thirties or forties, that suggests there is another aspect of ourselves that has yet to be disclosed and developed. Carl Jung said, " In the second half of our life, we turn our basic orientation of life from concern with opinions of others to concern with the being and growth of the self."

The minor details of our daily lives, to which we give the majority of our time, do not comprise the meaning of life. It is the inner vision and inner development of self that give our soul the freedom to soar unencumbered by the weight of our thoughts.

As you travel along your path, find a teacher; in fact, find several. We were not meant to journey through this second half of our lives alone.

INNER EXPLORATION

1. To prepare for this meditation, go to a place that gives to you the feeling of tranquility. You may find that in your garden, on a settee on your patio, sitting snugly in a cozy chair in front of your fireplace, or in your bathtub encircled with candles. Find your stillness within.

2. Relax and enjoy reading the meditation. Receive the meaning of each sentence of this meditation slowly, consciously.

   I turn away from the noise of the world around me to the world of silence that lies within me. I breathe the breath that my heart would have me breathe. I breathe the breath that activates the original blueprint of my soul. I shut out all memories that are linked to the past. I create no images of the future. I focus on what my life is telling me now.

In this space, I am aware that Who I Am is a part of All That Is, and in that I find my repose. I connect my Spirit to the consciousness of the one Divine Spirit—God. In this consciousness, I am aware that there is only one heart beating, the heart of all life, and I am an important beat in this Divine heart.

I am not, nor ever will be, a victim of circumstance, for that is the role of the mind. The pure intentions of my heart are always made manifest through my unwavering faith in Divine Spirit. I surrender my ego, all doubts, all worries, all fear, all anger, and bask in the light of courage, faith, trust, and surrender.

From that place, I become pure love, fused with the Great Universal Love—for there is only one of us. As I bring forth my love for myself, I cannot help but feel loved, for all things are One. I perceive the magnificence of Who I Am and commit to assisting others in seeing their magnificence. I express my life in laughter and joy, in integrity, and in service. I add upon myself only the good, the great, the constructive, the whole, and the holiness. Nothing else is allowed into my Divine blueprint, and I am grateful to know where to find myself.

3. When you finish reading the words, stay in your still-point and breathe from the center of your heart. Listen only to the reverberation of the words. Listen.

4. Copy this meditation and give it to a loved one. Create sacred space with another and repeat this meditation together. Then stay together afterwards in the stillness. Pass the meditation along to others you know and invite them to do the same.

5. Write your own meditation from your heart. Begin the practice of daily stillness, daily meditation.

~~~~~~~~~

PRAYER IS PART OF INTENTION

While meditation is the place we go to *listen* to God, prayer is where we go to *talk* to God. Prayer is the opportunity to express to God whatever is within us. If we don't express what is within us, we will suffocate from the resulting silence. Meditation and prayer create a direct connection to God. Listening and speaking create a balance in communication with God.

When we speak or pray to God, we bring grace into our lives. The very name *God* instills within us a certainty that we can transcend the limitations of the human condition. In our prayers, we have the ability, inexplicably, to link up to a greater, more loving, and compassionate Intelligence. To forge this relationship with God, it's important to learn how to pray. Earlier, when I spoke of arriving at integrity through intention, I also spoke about the necessity of having faith that the unseen will receive your intention and the intention will manifest.

If we speak the words in prayer, but don't believe in the power of our prayer, we send a weakened message. When we pray a prayer that is limited in its scope by what we believe, we will find ourselves in despair. Prayer and meditation allow us to pierce the veil that we believe divides heaven and earth. For me, prayer delivers me into the gentle arms of a loving God who I *know* responds in ways that are always for my highest good. Prayer is a place where I can always find my center and use it for the highest good of myself and others.

The sole reason for prayer is to align our thoughts, emotions, and feelings with the will of the Divine. It is this alignment that allows for spiritual transformation. It creates the alchemy that bridges the gap between the seen and the unseen. Prayers of surrender yield great results. Prayers of gratitude, *no matter what things look like,* have mystical powers to transform current circumstances.

There were times along my path when I misunderstood prayer, but then I misunderstood God, and, sadly, misunderstood myself as well. I railed against God when things didn't go my way, and I called that prayer. I asked for things that I believed would set me free, and I thought that was prayer. I begged for peace, and I thought that was prayer. I demanded that my intentions be made manifest *now,* and called that prayerful request. I believed inwardly that I didn't deserve happiness, yet I demanded that God secure it for me, and I thought that was prayer. Prayer is not a place we go with a list of demands. Without love, there is no prayer, and without the alignment of our thoughts, feelings, emotions, words, and deeds (integrity), our prayers are not heard and are ineffective.

The prayer that Jesus always spoke was, in essence, "Thank you, God, for already solving this problem for me." Then he let it go. He never had to ask for anything because, in spiritual reality, he knew he already had everything that he could possibly want or need. We, too, already have everything. Jesus was sent here to be the example of human capability. But we separated ourselves from him and considered him our Savior, not our example—and missed the entire point of his life. We went on to misunderstand who we truly are and what we are capable of, thus missing the point of our own lives. Our lack of understanding of who we truly are and the power we have within us causes us to believe we lack or need. It is our *belief* in lack that *causes* lack. It is our lack of integrity and imagination that turns prayer into pleading.

Prayer was never meant to be a request; it was intended to create a bond with God and align our will with God's will. Then, together, we are able to create the intended outcome. In the 1950s, a mystic named Neville wrote eight books with one common thread: imagination. He suggested that for a wish to be fulfilled, we need only close our eyes, quiet our bodies, align our emotions, feelings, and thoughts, and experience in our imagination the manifestation of the wish fulfilled.

I have had many people tell me that their prayers have gone unanswered, and I used to feel the same way. I used to tell my best friend that God must be on vacation because God certainly wasn't listening to a word I had to say! And then I came to understand why.

When we consider the wisdom of Jesus and the mysticism of Neville, we see that prayer cannot be answered if we are praying through a clouded consciousness. In *The Isaiah Effect,* author Gregg Braden revealed a lost mode of prayer he discovered in his study of the Dead Sea Scrolls. He cautions us: "Should fear, doubt, anxiety, or worry be in any way present in our prayers, we have lost the entrainment

[alignment] of our thoughts, our emotions, and our feelings."
In other words, when we have not lined up the dynamics
required for prayer, no message is sent. We often pray when
fear has enveloped us in a web of darkness. Our thoughts
turn to God for help when we feel helpless and our emotions
are in distress. At those times, there is no alignment.

As I retrace the footsteps of my life, I can see the divinity
in every single dilemma I created for myself. Through my
desire to live my life with integrity and see the larger picture, each difficulty has led me to a greater understanding
of Who I Am. So now when I am faced with a challenge,
regardless of what it is, I immediately turn to God and give
thanks for the situation. Then I surrender it. That is not to
say that as a spiritual being in the process of having a human experience I don't revisit the dilemma in moments of
fear—I do. But before I get lost in my mind's chatter, I catch
myself and go back again to give thanks and to surrender
everything that is necessary for the situation to unfold. That
is how I pray. Ugo Betti, in his book *Struggle Till Dawn,* said,
"When you want to believe in something, you also have to
believe in everything that's necessary for believing in it."

I will forever be thankful for the following story which I
heard Oprah Winfrey share.

As a child, her favorite book was The Color Purple, *by Alice
Walker. She carried that book with her everywhere and read it
dozens of times. When she heard that Steven Spielberg was going
to adapt the book into a film and was auditioning actors for the
roles, Oprah decided she had to be in that movie. It seemed meant
to be because one of the main characters was a man named Harpo,
which is her name spelled backwards.*

*A virtual unknown at the time, Oprah tried out for the part
of Harpo's wife, Sofia. She went home and waited—and heard*

nothing. She could think of nothing else but getting that role. Praying didn't appear to be helping. She decided to go to a health spa and lose some weight, thinking that maybe then she would have a better chance of getting the role. She was working out when an old gospel hymn called "I Surrender" came into her mind. She began singing that song with all her heart and soul. She meant it. Right then and there, she decided to stop thinking about the part, stop wanting it so much, and just surrender the outcome to God. Literally within minutes, one of the administrators of the spa found her and said, "Ms. Winfrey, Steven Spielberg is on the phone for you." Needless to say, she got the role and she learned how to truly pray for her intended outcome.

When we see no light at the end of the tunnel, we look to God to solve our dilemma, seldom understanding that the dilemma itself is the Divine at work. There is something to be learned from the problem, and if our prayer is one of surrender, and not geared to outcome, we will be lifted and guided to an illumined answer.

Prayer for me is a daily greeting to God in the morning and a good night to God in the evening. I am always acknowledging God throughout the day in prayers of gratitude. I truly doubt that God wants to hear from us only when we need something. I'm sure God wants to hear good news, too, or just be acknowledged and loved. And I know for sure that my seesaw works much better with God on the other side!

INNER EXPLORATION

1. I wrote the following prayer to add to my morning prayers. Consider praying this prayer to the God of your knowing each morning. Once inspired, consider writing your own special morning prayer.

Dear God,

Thank you for every blessing and for every awareness that has been brought to my life. Thank you for each moment of the day that lies before me, allowing me to create my greatest expression of love. Thank you for the opportunity to see familiar, loving faces today, that I may express my love and gratitude to them. Thank you for new and unfamiliar people and opportunities that may appear today, bringing me greater insight into myself.

May this day bring forth a freedom in my soul that I did not know yesterday. May this day remind me to be strong and compassionate. May this day show me my own courage. I ask for the outpouring of Your love on every creature large and small that lives upon the back of Mother Earth. Please open my own heart even further that I may be an expression of the outpouring of Your love to all of humankind. May Your light be the Light in me, and may it shine undeniably wherever I am today.

Thank you very much.

There is great freedom and a deep connection to the universal pulse when we live our lives with Integrity, the third aspect of BLISS. When we commit ourselves to emancipation from an inner world riddled with duality, we are on our way to experiencing the Oneness, the bliss that is intended for us all.

CHAPTER 4

Sexuality

*I want this music and this dawn
and the warmth of your cheek against mine*
—Rumi, Sufi poet

Experiencing and expressing our sexuality and honoring its sacredness play a great part in our journey to bliss. Our sexuality is intricately enmeshed with our minds, emotions, physical well-being, and spirituality. Understanding the Divinity of our sexuality and the pure power of our sacred sexual energy will open our hearts, allow us to come ever closer to the heart of God (where love is real, rather than an illusion), and arrive at a more meaningful experience of pure love.

The first "S" in the acronym BLISS stands for **sexuality** and **sensuality**, which I regard as being as intimately linked as integrity and intention. Sexuality without sensuality is not the genuine article.

People too often dispense with sensuality and think of sexuality as merely one's approach or physical appeal in the pursuit and bedding of another. Sexuality is frequently lost under the layers of clothing, makeup, and cavalier attitudes that we believe exemplify our sexual essence. It is most often buried deep beneath the stories of our lives, the lovers that have come and gone, and a heart that refuses to ache or bleed again because of past experience.

In reality, sexuality is what enables us to live fully, to take in such exquisiteness that we bloom open to that which is God—pure love. Spirituality is God essence expressed in the soul. Sexuality is God essence expressed in physicality.

In the previous chapters on Balance, Love, and Integrity, I discussed at length the importance of deepening each, which propels us closer to experiencing bliss. **Sexuality**, the fourth element in our journey, is the ongoing process of coming to know ourselves, and love and honor ourselves, in a somewhat different way. It is about self-discovery in relationship to our body, a partner, and all of life. With the awareness and practiced strategies of balance, love, and integrity more firmly rooted within us, our ability to experience our full sexuality will be greatly enhanced.

This chapter explores what holds us back from the full experience of our sexuality, how we can remove those obstacles, and how we can support and nourish our sexuality.

SEXUALITY AND RELATIONSHIPS ARE DIVINE GIFTS

Someone once said (my apologies to the author for not remembering who you are): "Sexuality is a doorway to the ecstatic mind of great bliss." It is natural for us to experience our sexuality as a free-flowing, joyful energy that opens us to the natural state of bliss inherent in everyone.

Enjoying our sexuality to its fullest potential requires us to bring into harmony all of our bodies—our emotional, mental, spiritual, and physical bodies. We operate on our highest level of consciousness when our hearts are fully open and we honor and revere all of our bodies. We experience our greatest sexual and spiritual orgasm when we are completely openhearted and all of our bodies are in balance. We assimilate and create the greatest qualities of life with an open heart and when all of our bodies are unified in their energy.

Full acceptance and loving embrace of ourselves includes accepting and loving our magnificent living organism, the body. *A Course in Miracles* says, "The body is a tiny fence around a little part of a glorious and complete idea." If any part of us is taken up with the energy of criticism, self-hatred, self-loathing, or self-deprecation, then the energy running through the body is in conflict, and the spirit's full expression of sexuality and love is diminished.

The factors that most influence our sexuality are our emotions and what we think about ourselves. Our emotions affect us on a daily basis and drive our relationships, with self and others, to success or failure. Most of us spend our lifetime coming to terms with our emotional wounds from childhood and past relationships. That is life's opportunity, not its sentence. In every relationship we enter, we have an opportunity to heal our wounds, for it is through our relationships that we become aware of our true emotional condition. This is true of all of our relationships, not just those with a lover or life partner. Every relationship allows us to witness our own interactions, responses, and behaviors.

We don't truly know who we are in relationship until we are in one. When it comes to a partner, for instance, it's easy to be in the comfort of our own home and tell ourselves that we have changed. We might believe that we are no longer a jealous or angry person, that we're not needy, and we're emotionally available to be in a partner relationship. It's easy when we're tired of being alone to tell ourselves that we're willing to love another unconditionally, or that we're willing to negotiate the differences between our life and our partner's life.

But when it comes down to it, it is not easy or simple to live in the present with a fully open, trusting heart, undaunted by the past, and committed to devotional surrender to a partner we have yet to meet, or the one that currently shares our bed.

In relationship with another, we learn things about ourselves that we may not have discovered or admitted before. If we move our egos aside and become a conscious observer while in relationship, we will notice that the relationship brings to the surface every unhealed emotion from the past. We will see that what is necessary to the health of the relationship is what is required for our own spiritual growth. It is our responsibility to tone our emotional muscles and open wide our hearts to better support a new relationship entering our lives, or to invigorate an already existing one.

RELEASING THE TRAPPINGS OF THE PAST

I have spoken at length about the ego and mind keeping us from the truth about ourselves, keeping us off balance. We are unable to enjoy the bliss of our sexuality and the freedom of a fully open heart when we allow the voices from the past, which have turned into our current voice, to continue to hit "replay." Old thought patterns do not give us the freedom to experience the truth of who we really are. If we don't have a deep sense of who we are, how will our partner know who we are? Or how will we be able to attract the depth and expansiveness we desire in a partner? For, according to Universal Law, we can only attract our likeness, our reciprocal. If we're still trapped in our history, listening to our old tapes and outdated judgments, we will draw in someone who is doing the same, and neither partner will be clear on who they truly are. Who we think we are is often a misguided part of ourselves making up who we think we should be.

To express who we are is to be who we are *now*. It requires no more than showing up, wide open from your deepest heart, and allowing yourself to be vulnerable in order to experience yourself fully alive.

Thomas Merton wrote: "The only true joy on earth is to escape from the prison of our own false self, and enter by love into union with the Life who dwells within the essence of every creature and in the core of our own souls."

When I was growing up, my stepmother told me more than once, "You will never amount to anything and nobody will ever want you." I believed her. As an adult, when it came to men, I always kept myself in what I believed to be a position of control, so my stepmother's prediction would never have a chance to come true. I never completely surrendered my heart, which I thought protected me from the hurt of a man not wanting me. I had no idea then how thick the layers surrounding my heart—my connection to all that is Life—had become. A statement made over twenty years before was the belief system I lived with, daily.

In spite of that, I never had trouble attracting men. Unconsciously, I weeded out the ones that might force me to open my heart and kept the ones who were "safe." Regardless of safety, I had trouble believing the men were genuinely interested in me. I knew they were interested in me sexually, but sexually interested was a far cry from genuinely interested, and being good in bed was a long way from connecting with my sexuality. I routinely suspected them of cheating on me (even if they weren't), and eventually found an escape route with each one in case he was thinking of leaving me first. When one would say he loved me (and more than one did) I would respond with an incredulous "You do?" And then I would ask myself how that was possible. How could he love somebody who was unlovable? How could he love somebody who was ashamed of herself and the family she had been born to?

I finally began to see the light one morning at 3 a.m. At the time, I was dating a well-known, very attractive actor. It shouldn't surprise you that we lived in different states—perfect for somebody like me who loved distance. And of course, I was always wondering what a famous person who could date virtually anybody could possibly see in me. He was in New York when he called me in Arizona, so there was a three-hour time difference. I was in a sound sleep when the phone rang. When I answered, he said, "I know it's late, but I just wanted to tell you something."

"What?" I asked, sleepily.

"I love you." This was the first time he'd said that to me.

I bolted upright in bed and replied immediately with my usual incredulity. "You do?"

"Yes, I do, and I can't wait to see you this weekend."

When I hung up the phone, I couldn't go back to sleep. I decided to attempt to understand what this really wonderful man loved about me. Or for that matter, what had any man in my *past who told me he loved me seen in me? The tape in my head told me I wasn't lovable, nobody would ever want me.*

I turned on the lamp, found a piece of paper and a pen in the nightstand drawer, and wrote, "What is it about me that makes me lovable?" (I had already made it quite clear to myself what didn't make me lovable, according to my judgment system.) Here is what I came up with:

I'm really a lot of fun to be with.

I'm thoughtful and giving.

I love children.

I love animals.

I respect the wisdom of elders.

I'm a good conversationalist.

I'm a generous and exciting lover.

I'm cute and sexy.

I make people in my life feel special, and I know that's important.

I listen with real interest.

Other people's feelings matter to me.

There's something inside me that shines brighter than what my stepmother said about me.

I'm a good person.

I have a big heart.

I AM a child of God. It is my Divine birthright to be loved.

Making this list was the beginning of ripping out the trappings of my past and becoming current with the truth of myself.

INNER EXPLORATION

1. For this exploration, go to a place in your home that is nurturing to you. Set up a tape recorder with a blank tape. When you are ready, take seven deep breaths. Bring your awareness into the center of your heart and ask yourself, "What is it about me that makes me lovable?" *Feel* your own lovableness.

2. Record your answers on the tape and write them down in your journal as well.

3. Breathe again, deeply. Breathe in your lovableness. Be with your lovableness. Witness the experience of this revelation about yourself. Witness the freedom that truth provides you.

4. For the next three months, listen to the tape every evening just before you go to sleep. Tuck it in with you at night. Sleep well!

SHAME AND GUILT BLOCK SEXUALITY

It's not possible to express our sexuality honestly and ultimately when we are playing victim to shame and guilt from our daily judgment about days gone by. Shame and guilt are barriers that keep true love and sexual freedom from arriving at their destination—our hearts. Shame and guilt affect our behavior in relationships. They limit our ability to be devoted to any relationship—be it with self or other. They prevent us from living the full spectrum of our sexuality, which can only happen with a completely open, softened heart. Shame and guilt can also perpetuate a false sense of sexiness that is often mistaken for healthy sexuality. Shame and guilt are the culprits that convince us to settle for less than the Divine intended.

Shame

Shame is a judgment that we placed upon ourselves in connection with an experience in the past. Shame carries with it feelings of inferiority, avoidance of real commitment, and a need to be perfect that often turns into performance anxiety. We spend a great deal of time trying to be something that doesn't exist—perfect—and when we can never attain this perfection, we reject ourselves. If we cannot transform our self-rejection into self-love, we will never know our true nature nor realize the very purpose for being: love. As long as we reject ourselves, we will never feel accepted by others.

I once asked a client to share with me the most shameful thing she was holding onto, something she couldn't leave behind and which plagued her. When she told me and I didn't react, except to treat her lovingly, she was shocked and then relieved. Usually, what we feel shame over will have little or no effect on someone close to us whom we choose to tell. There is something in the telling of it to someone we trust, whose only purpose is to hold the space of loving energy without judgment, that begins to dissolve the shame. It is our silence and our judgment about the experience that has enlarged our shame to astounding proportions. We have turned the experience into the monster under the bed.

Please know that your particular monster is not unique. Many people have monsters that look like yours. We all share experiences that are similar in the shame they produce. The details of these experiences are merely variations on a theme. It's important to note, however, that it is the way in which we decide to view the experience that produces the shame. If we can regard our behavior and what happens to us with loving forgiveness, it will lead us out of the personal hell of shame.

Guilt

Please write down the following sentence and post it in a place where you will see it daily:

Part of the human experience is to make mistakes.

Making a mistake does not automatically make us guilty of anything. In considering guilt, it's necessary to understand the difference between *healthy* guilt and *neurotic* guilt. Healthy guilt is our conscience telling us we are doing something morally wrong, that we are acting against our belief system or value system. Remembering something we did in the past that hurt others or ourselves is important in order to keep us from inflicting pain again.

Neurotic guilt is feeling bad about something about which there is no moral reason to feel bad or guilty. It can be as simple as feeling guilty over missing a good friend's birthday party because you weren't feeling particularly well. Or it can be more complex, as when you feel guilty (or terrible about yourself) that your house wasn't in perfect condition when your mother came to visit, and you know hers would have been spotless. Neurotic guilt wrecks havoc in our lives. It's rarely about what actually occurs. It's most often about internalized judgments from the past. It becomes a punishment that we inflict upon ourselves, often without realizing it, and the ramifications deplete our life force.

Neurotic guilt frequently causes people to choose a partner who does not embrace the sacredness of partnership. This is because neurotic guilt carries with it self-involvement and lack of self-worth—remember, in relationships, we draw in our reciprocal. Neurotic guilt leads to molding our lives around someone else's needs, clinging to another, feeling desperate about the relationship, obsessing about the other person, constructing a false image of that person—all of which further damages the psyche.

Neurotic guilt may create physical "dis-ease" (which is not being at ease in the body) as a result of loveless thinking. Those enmeshed in neurotic guilt may find financial stability elusive. They may also become celibate or impotent, be prone to angry outbursts, and unconsciously elicit physical or emotional abuse from others. In any case, neurotic guilt is guaranteed to keep us from the blissful stage of sexuality.

Childhood abuse or neglect often produces neurotic guilt in the victim. (I use the word 'victim' only in cases of childhood abuse or neglect.) Those who have endured such experiences typically have an inappropriate understanding of sexuality and are incapable of dissolving unhealthy bound-aries in order to receive love without fear. As a partner, they often diminish and distort their sexuality with aggressive or passive-aggressive behavior. They may unconsciously view their partners as parents and the resulting displaced anger prevents the body and the heart from opening fully.

Neurotic guilt will not allow wonderful relationships to enter our lives. The heart's yearnings go unrecognized and are replaced by a lifestyle filled with activities and busy-ness that tricks us into believing that our hearts are full. The heart, through which the soul speaks, is desirous of experi-encing ecstasy on a physical level, so that we may know a much grander ecstasy on a soul level. The soul and the body share in the oneness that is God.

Bliss cannot be attained by living in the past. Guilts of the past must be given voice to someone we trust, be deeply forgiven, and allowed to leave. The beauty of the past, every past, is that we each have an opportunity to make our lives more valuable now. Our past teaches us what works well for our lives and what does not. With that knowledge, we can take our place in the "Now" and live in a way that fulfills ourselves and others. We can be restored to our original nature if we allow ourselves to be.

If you have unfinished business with the past, now is the time to get rid of it. Be honest with yourself about what's still lingering in the hallways of your life. If you're harbor-ing neurotic guilt, you will find it impossible to enter into the free flow of your life and allow your heart the openness necessary to experience your sexuality in a blissful way. Make a decision to let go of guilt, and have the courage to get on with your life.

Forgiveness: The Fire Extinguisher for Shame and Guilt

Shame and guilt turn to loathing of self and others, which renders us incapable of experiencing spiritual maturity, sexual maturity, and true intimacy. In this way, shame and guilt deplete us of our natural power to be glorious, radiant, and whole.

I rarely, if ever, encounter a new client who is not still being pulled down by shame and guilt from the past. For almost all of those who seek my help, the past has caused a severe power outage in their current lives. At our first meeting, most of my clients variously cite their dysfunctional family, parents, or ex-partners as the source of their problems. I suggest to them that on this day they make a decision to call back their power. In our work together, I assist them in becoming aware of the fact that, during all the years that they put the onus on their biological or step-family, ex-husband, ex-wife, or ex-lover, little in their internal life changed. They soon realize that very little in their external life changed either, with the exception of natural life occurrences, the comings and goings of people and jobs that happen with the passage of time. That adds up to not much more than a lateral move, and much less than spiritual success.

The shame and guilt that are impeding their lives and loves, I remind them, will continue to be there, hovering like dark clouds on a gray day, until they understand that forgiveness is the only action that extinguishes shame and guilt and restores the power they have knocked out. *A Course in Miracles* says, "The holiest of all spots on earth is where an ancient hatred has become a present love."

INNER EXPLORATION

1. Approach this inner exploration with deep honesty and reverent compassion for yourself. With your awareness in the center of your heart, answer the following questions, writing your answers in your journal.

2. Regarding Shame:

   (a) What do I still feel shame about?

   (b) Who do I trust to tell what I feel shame about? (Later, when you are ready, tell that person about the incidents connected to your shame. If there is no one you trust, tell God, and feel the presence of love without judgment enfold you.)

   (c) How is this shame affecting my life and my choices now?

   (d) Who am I apart from this shame?

   (e) Am I willing and ready to acknowledge that whatever I have called shameful is now over and done with, and the holding onto it serves no useful purpose? Am I willing to stop having my life run by what I have judged to be shameful? In other words, are you ready to get on with your life, or is this shame you are hanging on to providing you with an excuse to not move on and be All That You Can Be? This is a very important question. There is no room for anything here but complete and total honesty.

3. Regarding Guilt:

   (a) What am I feeling guilty about? (List all.)

   (b) Which of my guilts are healthy guilts and which are neurotic guilts?

   (c) Did I know better at the time when I made the choices I made? (Answer for each guilt.)

   (d) Do any of my guilts call for atonement?

   (e) What are the steps I will take immediately to atone for the choices that are causing me to feel healthy guilt, so that I can move on with my life? (Take those actions as soon as possible. Without action, your answer to this question is meaningless.)

   (f) Am I willing to make healthy, moral decisions for the highest good of all concerned from this day forward so as not to create any further guilt?

   (g) Am I ready to release neurotic guilt? Is carrying guilt around with me something that I find necessary in order to remind myself to be a kind, loving, thoughtful, compassionate, sensual person? Am I not all of those things simply by my nature?

4. This important step will take you time to do deeply and authentically. It is essential to understand the magnitude and power of forgiveness. It is not as difficult to forgive as it is to stay angry and stuck. Ben Franklin said, "Whatever is begun in anger, ends in shame."

   Forgiveness is an act of the heart that requires nothing more than a decision to no longer live in the past. Forgiveness is the ultimate act of compassion.

It takes care of unfinished emotional business and preserves your emotional well-being. It stops you from being bonded to someone through fear and it binds you to Life—with love. Forgiveness is self-love that lifts you above pain and gives you freedom.

Forgive yourself for believing things that others said to you that caused neurotic guilt in you. Forgive the people who said those things to you. Forgive the things you did and the choices you made that were not formed with the highest good of all concerned in mind. Forgive yourself for staying loyal to your old patterns of thinking.

Over time you will find you no longer give forgiveness, you become forgiveness.

5. With the release of shame and guilt, you can reclaim your power! You have just been given a "Get Out of Jail Free" card. Recreate your life. With intentions fully in place, be prepared to be guided by Spirit.

~~~~~~~~~

Choosing a Partner

Gamble everything for love...
Half-Heartedness doesn't reach into majesty
You set out to find God,
but then you keep stopping for long periods
at mean-spirited roadhouses.
Don't wait any longer.
Dive in the ocean,
leave and let the sea be you...

—Rumi

The choice we make in a partner will either make us feel good about ourselves and our sexuality, or support us in the further robbing of both. The choice will also either bring us closer to or take us further from God. When Rumi wrote about getting deterred by stopping at "mean-spirited road-houses," he was reminding us to stop making poor choices that keep us from our Divine joy!

To revitalize our lives and sexuality, we must honor ourselves, and choose a partner who will provide us with opportunities to expand the awareness of who we are and gain more unity with God. Whether we are able to do this depends upon which aspects of ourselves we allow to do the choosing: the personality and the ego, or the heart and soul.

The Point of View of the Personality and Ego

When we view love from the perspective of the personality and ego, we look for love outside ourselves. We are either gloriously excited about a new love, disillusioned with an old one, turning to our friends for commiseration when love ends, or desperately searching for love. We boldly claim one minute that we don't need a relationship, and the next finds us battling with depression over lack of love.

When we view love from the perspective of the personality and ego, we expect another person to fill the void within us. When that doesn't occur, the personality and ego experience pain, resentment, and bitterness. We then build a fortress around our heart and create a fractured sense of Self.

The personality is formed of those splintered parts of the soul that have emerged to take on experience and require healing in this lifetime. The ego is I/me/mine and uses the personality to further its ends, cheering on the personality and thereby according it a falsely elevated status. The ego tries to ensure our happiness by keeping everything under tight control. The acronym for EGO is Edging God Out. With the ego running things, deep soul connection, and therefore true happiness, is not possible.

Although our focus may remain steadily on love, our perception of what love is tends to be incorrect because it reflects the point of view of the ego and personality, rather than that of the heart and soul. The personality's urge is for champagne, roses, constant attention, and complete understanding. These great expectations set us up for failure in relationships. In an attempt to protect itself from the slings and arrows of love, the ego sets up scenarios that keep a mild level of misery running through our lives.

The ego uses relationships as a means to fulfill needs as the personality defines them. Perhaps what the personality needs is not to be alone anymore, so the ego settles for whoever is available. Perhaps the personality is desperate to feel loved, so the ego promotes being sexual with someone too quickly in an attempt to achieve that—and the light of day brings the painful realization that love had nothing to do with the encounter. When holidays loom, the personality wants a partner for the festivities. Desperation, rather than consciousness, drives the search for someone with whom to go to parties, exchange gifts, share a bottle of champagne, and usher in the new year. If we are already in a relationship, the personality and ego start expecting of our partner a certain kind of behavior, which coincides with the holiday time of year, not the condition of the heart.

These superficial standards for a relationship are often the reason we attract people into our lives who don't really want us. We don't really want them, either. We want what they can give to us on a superficial level. We want immediate gratification. We call forth someone to do things for us or with us, and to fill a void not meant to be filled by another. When we do this, we aren't heeding the call of the heart and soul by calling forth deep love or opening ourselves deeply to love. We aren't inviting a beloved into our lives to bring forth the maximal opportunity for our mutual spiritual growth. Instead, our ego and personality want a dinner partner and a bedmate.

When we choose a partner in this way, sooner or later we come to realize that this is not a person we can trust. We realize that although we are not alone, we're still lonely and unfulfilled. If we're lucky, it will finally dawn on us that we have loved ourselves too little, again, and we will decide to treat ourselves with more dignity.

The Point of View of the Heart and Soul

Like the personality and ego, the heart and soul are unified in their point of view. Their desire to be in an honoring, intimate, illumined, loving, conscious, communicative, nurturing relationship with another is a deep urge like no other. Their urge for a relationship is much different from the urge of the personality and ego. The heart and soul desire true relationship, which means true connection, so we can experience joy, the effervescence of life within us. The heart and soul desire for us to have another person who can serve as a Divine mirror to reflect facets of ourselves that we need to see in order to heal. Ascended Master St. Germain said (via channels Azena Ramanda and Claire Heartsong), "The meaning of relationship is merely the recognition of you in circumstance."

The heart and soul desire a relationship so that our individuated spirits can be opened more deeply to our true nature by merging in physicality the feminine and masculine aspects of all of creation—and thus experience re-union, or wholeness. Both genders carry within them both the masculine and feminine aspects. When we merge masculine and feminine energy through the physical body, opening the heart as the channel through which unconditional love travels, we have the supreme opportunity of experiencing our true nature: humility balanced with sovereignty. Feminine balanced with masculine. Love for the other, love for self. In a trusting, intimate, sacred relationship, we are able to open deeper, wider, and even beyond where our own imaginations can take us. It is through this merging and openness that we unify the God essence, the oneness within. There, the spark of life called passion is ignited.

The heart and soul understand that there is no separation between spirituality and sexuality. The specific urges of honor, intimacy, consciousness, nurturing, and other noble impulses are to help us become more aware of the need for a deeper heart connection and bring us back to our Divine self. It is through this understanding of the Divine purpose for relationship that the heart and soul assist us in choosing and accepting our partners in a more conscious way.

The Need for Reflection

In the space between our relationships, we need to be still and reflect, to request and open to the Wisdom greater than ourselves for help in seeing more clearly what caused us to call forth the experience we just had. Self-inquiry enables us to discover the selfish determinations that summoned the experience. We can illuminate the fears or needs we were harboring, which allowed the desires of the ego and personality to win out over the desires of the heart and soul in choosing a relationship. This is not a time for judgment, however, only reflection.

Through all my years of working with singles and couples, I have been continually astounded at what people *do not* take away from their previous relationships. When I ask men what happened in their last relationship, they generally tell me they don't know but, they are ready to move on with somebody better. When I ask women, most respond with, "He was just the wrong guy who didn't turn out the way I thought he would," followed by, "I'm tired of being hurt."

If you take umbrage with any of your past relationships, do not lose sight of the fact that you *chose* them. Every single one of them! Ask yourself honestly why you chose each and every person who was or still is significant in your life. It will give you great insight into yourself. Then ask yourself if you saw the end in the very beginning however, because your ego and personality had their own agenda, you wanted to participate in that relationship anyway. We are each responsible for the outcomes of our relationships by our decision to be in them.

Perhaps you chose a particular relationship because you were attracted to a person's "bad boy" or "bad girl" side. What would you expect the outcome to be? Perhaps you chose them thinking they would change. That is always a mistake. We do not possess the power to change anyone, except ourselves. Perhaps you chose someone because he or she had money, which led you to believe that you would find stability—another mistake. Someone else's money and your stability have nothing to do with each other.

Perhaps you chose someone for no apparent reason, but looking back you can see the perfection of that choice at that time in your life, how the other person reflected an aspect of yourself that needed to be examined and healed. Perhaps you chose someone because you were attracted at the time to a part of that person that you seemed to have lost in yourself.

Not all relationships are meant to last indefinitely. Some last for a season, some for a lifetime, but all arrive in our lives for a reason—to show us something more about ourselves.

Sometimes the Divine Chooses for Us

One of my employees and I were traveling to San Francisco on business. I always ask for my seat assignment in advance because I like to sit near the front of the plane in an aisle seat. When we checked in, however, I discovered that they had given me my aisle seat, but it was in the second to last row of the plane. Instead of requesting a different seat, I chose to believe there was a reason for the reassignment.

We took our seats. I began discussing business with my employee, Tonya, who had the aisle seat across from me. While the passengers were still boarding, I met the eyes of a young man as he was walking toward his seat behind Tonya. I wasn't initially attracted to him, but I had a sense that I would talk with him during the trip. Tonya and I talked for the next forty-five minutes, at which point the young man broke into our conversation.

He and I talked for the rest of the trip. He lived in San Francisco, he told me, but spent half of the month living in Phoenix, where he was opening a new restaurant. He asked me if I would like to go hiking with him in two weeks when he returned to Phoenix. I said yes, even though I wasn't attracted to him in the way I was "normally" attracted to men I date. I had the sense that this was a good thing for a change.

Immediately in his favor, he demonstrated responsibility, intelligence, and family values, all qualities I admire, and he was easy to talk to. He had a lightness to his spirit that appealed to me, since I had begun feeling heavy in my own spirit with the workload I had at that time, as well as dealing with the intensity of my inner healing work. I was leaving little or no room in my life for play, and was out of balance in a big way.

My knowingness led me to believe that a Power greater than myself carefully orchestrated this unplanned seating arrangement. When we got off the plane, he asked if we could get together while I was in San Francisco. I told him that I didn't have the time; it would be three days of a lot of work.

He called me two weeks later in Phoenix. Truthfully, I had given him little thought due to my busy schedule. Since I had said yes to a date, I honored my agreement. We went out to the lake and went on a wonderful hike. It was nice to be out in nature and feel lighter. I appreciated his ability to balance his heavy workload with play. He was ten years younger than I was, and there was something about his youthful exuberance that made me miss my own. I went out with him three times before I became aware of the real purpose of our meeting, and began to be really attracted to him. He brought a sense of freedom back to me, a sense of play and spontaneity, something that was buried somewhere beneath my workload, my spiritual work, and my efforts to survive. That was the attraction. That was the reason God had arranged our meeting. And I was going to honor that Divine arrangement and seek the ultimate fulfillment of this partnering for whatever time it was meant to stay.

I must tell you that during this time my sexuality soared, and so did his! We had a great time. The reason, and the beauty of the freedom, was that I had no delusions of this being anything other than what it was, and if it did turn out to be something else, it would get there when it got there. I was very much in the moment without expectations. What a concept! What an opportunity.

He enjoyed being exactly where he was in his life. He promised no commitment. By just being himself, he was giving me the opportunity to call back a lighter piece of myself that I was missing. I am blessed to have had the wisdom to recognize the opportunity and not confuse it with something else. We continued to enjoy our relationship for a time.

What ended it was another blessing. I realized that at the time I met him I was emotionally unavailable. He was also emotionally unavailable. The Divine mirror was showing me another part of myself. While dating him, I realized that emotional unavailability was a part of myself that I no longer wanted to experience. I had mastered that quite brilliantly. I decided to choose a different experience for myself. To expect him to change into someone emotionally available because I had made that choice for myself was not realistic. We discussed it at length, and he tried to the best of his ability to become more of what I was seeking. He was not ready, and so we parted. We remain good friends to this day.

We are all responsible for developing a deeper awareness of the sacredness of relationships and for getting to know ourselves well enough to understand why we choose our partners—whether for a season or for a lifetime. Trusting in the Divine to make some of the arrangements on our behalf serves us well. If we can do that, we will be able to move past the narcissistic preoccupation that too often accompanies the choosing of a partner. Trusting in the Divine also helps us to expand our hearts to encompass the life of another—for however long the experience was intended to last. If we cannot do that, we will only get what we give.

What this planet needs now is humans who are willing to rise to the occasion of being in a relationship for the purpose of opening wide the heart and merging the individual soul's light with that of another. The future of the planet depends upon the blossoming of this way of loving.

INNER EXPLORATION

1. Take this time to look at the last three relationships in your life. You may include the one you are in now, if you like. What has each of these relationships revealed to you about yourself?

2. What were the reasons you chose to be in each of these relationships?

3. What are the similarities in the outcomes of each of the past three relationships? If you are currently in a relationship, does this one mirror in any way the patterns of your past relationships, or do you see a difference?

4. What part of yourself do you miss—a part that you have given away or forgotten about—that you desire to bring back into your life?

5. Are you willing to become a partner who can trust, in order for you to choose a partner you can trust?

6. Are you willing to open your heart completely, to let somebody enter deep inside you, past your resistances, past your pain, past your past?

7. Are you able to let go of your fantasy partner in order to be in a relationship with a beloved who inspires you spiritually?

8. Write down the deepest desires that your heart and soul yearn for in a relationship. Post them somewhere that you can see them. With the awareness of your deepest yearnings, make a life decision not to be sidetracked by less.

~~~~~~~~

HONORING THE SACRED FEMININE WITHIN

Denying the sacred feminine within is another way that we limit our sexuality and close our hearts. As I said earlier, both genders carry both the feminine and masculine aspects of self. The feminine essence is the life force of love. It is magical and mystical, powerful and sweet. For many women, it has been difficult to come to terms with and honor their feminine aspect because of the societal and familial invalidation of feminine beliefs and values that haunt us. For many men, embracing the feminine within is equally difficult, if not more so, because of the societal and familial exhortations to "be a man!" It is this that has kept men and women from their hearts' deepest desires.

The feminine essence can no longer be invalidated unless we continue to believe that it can and act accordingly. If we do not reemerge and open ourselves to our sacred feminine—that which is spiritual, that which is love—our hearts' deepest yearnings will not be fulfilled.

Walt Whitman wrote: "Be not ashamed woman…You are the gates of the body, and you are the gates of the soul."

When a woman reclaims her sacred feminine self, a rebirthing takes place, and from that a woman emerges, magical and enchanting, magnetic and contagious. A woman unto herself can change the state of a man or a nation. The feminine essence is one of beauty and joy, compassion and nurturing—not loneliness, contention, and heartache. A woman unto herself does not use her feminine wiles to antagonize a man or to prove a point; she sacredly uses her body as an instrument of God for giving and receiving love.

This is a time like no other to embrace your sacred feminine self. The world is in need of women and men confident in their abilities to love and nurture—and who understand the power of the feminine aspect to open otherwise closed hearts. The sacred feminine essence fosters peace and serenity.

Where the sacred feminine is not allowed to express itself, the effects are evident. We see desperation, war-torn countries, the toppling of governments, divided rather than united people. We see imbalance and rage. We do not see love. We do not see a woman feeling or expressing as a woman. We do not see devotion in the eyes of men. We do not see families or communities held together by the love of women.

We have a mission, a Divine mission, that asks us to take responsibility for the gifts within us. As each of us embraces our sacred feminine, which is one of those gifts, individual wounds will heal, and relationships and eventually nations will be restored to that which God intended—unity of Spirit.

How, you may ask, do I get from where I am with all my pain to this loving, joyful woman or man? You do it one day at a time by detoxifying your past, and leading with your heart, not your mind. There is nothing you need to seek in the outer world to do this, for the flame of the sacred feminine is still burning within you, no matter how hard you have tried to extinguish or ignore the light. A good place to start reconnecting with the sacred feminine is in the five senses. Start to feel your way home one day at a time, one sense at a time.

COMING HOME TO THE SENSES

> Various types of nourishing and savory foods, and sweet, delicious, refreshing drinks, a conversation which is pleasing to the ears, and a light touch which caresses the skin. Clear nights, which are sweetened by the rays of a full moon...pleasant songs, which entrance and captivate the soul, the chewing of betel leaves, wine and garlands, sweetly scented flowers, and a happy and unencumbered heart—these are the best aphrodisiacs in life.
>
> —Susrata, Indian surgeon, 800 B.C.

Becoming intimate with your sense of taste, touch, smell, hearing, and sight does not necessitate being with a partner. Experiencing for yourself and giving to yourself assist you in understanding the needs of a beloved. The suffering in our relationships is usually due to disconnection from the self. If we can experience the intensity and sensitivity of our senses, we will be able to share this with our beloved. When we involve the five senses (sensuality) in our lovemaking, we create an atmosphere of romance and amplify our sexuality, which diminishes the risk of sex becoming an empty habit or a dull duty.

Tuning into each of our senses keeps us engaged and entwined by the present moment. When all of our senses are engaged, we come to know life and all of its particulars intimately. By heightening all of our senses, we make it possible to experience the pinnacle of sexuality.

The Sense of Taste

Taste is influenced by all of the other senses. The enhanced deliciousness of food eaten in an atmosphere bathed in candlelight. The sensuousness of putting food into your mouth or someone else's mouth. The influence of wonderful aromas. The sound of a champagne cork sending your taste buds into anticipation of champagne's cool sensual arrival in your mouth. The visual stimulation of Mother Nature's bounty.

The taste sensations of food are sensual and sexual. How often have we exclaimed over the taste of food in much the same fashion as we exclaim over wonderful lovemaking? "Oh, my God, this is good. This chocolate cake is amazing. This lobster is so juicy. That meal was so good last night, I'm still thinking about it. Mmmmm, this is the best red wine I've had in a long time."

Taste becomes even more sensual when we savor it lingeringly. There is a significant difference between the person who sits down to eat for the sake of eating and the one who sits down to have the experience of taste, even if it's Chinese take-out.

Remember, you do not need to have a partner to become intimate with your sense of taste, or to develop your appreciation of taste and what it does for you. Take note of each morsel that passes your lips or the liquid that glides down your throat as it satisfies your desire.

Once you've become aware of the sensuality of your taste and you are in a relationship with another, experience taste with your partner. How do his lips taste against the swell of your tongue, or his neck as your mouth makes its journey to pleasure? What do the tips of his fingers taste like as you slowly investigate each one with your mouth? What will you both experience as you join the nectar of food with the nectar of the body? I'm certain that you can imagine the difference that awareness—being conscious of each moment— makes in your experience of taste.

INNER EXPLORATION

To enjoy the intriguing, intimate bond between food and sexuality, first experiment and come to know your own heightened sense of taste.

1. Spend time carefully planning this experience. Create on your own (or go out with your partner or a friend) a spectacular, sensual meal with different textures and flavors in an atmosphere that appeals to all of your senses.

2. Slowly and deliberately savor every moment and every morsel of your experience. Become completely absorbed in what you taste and how you respond as a result of the experience.

3. Let this become a habit to replace the habitual experience of eating without tasting, without savoring, without being present in the moment.

~~~~~~~

The Sense of Touch

Touching is something we do every waking hour of our day. Most often we do so carelessly, not thoughtfully. If we were asked at day's end what we touched that day that pleased us most, we would most likely not know. We typically touch on automatic pilot. There are times I envy people employed at nurseries—both baby nurseries and plant nurseries. What they touch is obviously sacred and they touch with more reverence. In return, their touch gifts them with a feeling of connection and well-being.

When we consciously and lovingly touch another person, a pet, a plant, a flower, or a tree, the pituitary gland in our brain releases a hormone known as oxytocin. This hormone induces a state of pleasure and brings forth the feeling of satiation. Even the non-sexual touch between friends stimulates the release of oxytocin and contributes to the healing of our sense of separation.

You can tell a lot about a person by the way they hug. To be held in a heart-to-heart embrace, even for a brief moment, conveys a feeling of connection. That moment of heart connection allows you to feel oneness. It is far different from having someone barely touch you when they hug. I have become well aware of my emotional and bodily reactions to both kinds of hugs. The absent-hearted hugger always leaves me feeling disconnected, whereas the person who really hugs me consciously brings warmth into my heart and that person lingers with me throughout the day, and often into the next.

Our touch holds tremendous power. It has the power to heal, the power to convey genuine care, and the power to transmit love. No other sense contributes more to sexual pleasure than touch. When we make love, it is only through touch that we can experience intense pleasure. Our highest level of ecstasy is not in orgasm, but in the way we are touched in the process leading up to the orgasm. The human body has more than forty-five miles of nerve endings in it. The more touching you engage in that is not directly sexual, the more sexually romantic will be the response.

I was having dinner with a new friend last year, and he asked me, "Why are you holding your own hand?" I was completely unaware that during our conversation I had both arms on the table with one hand cupping the other. I offhandedly said I wasn't aware that I had been, but it felt good to have my hand held. He took my hand in his and asked me if that felt better. My response was, "Not better, but different." All touch is soothing.

Throughout the week, I thought about him bringing my hand-holding to my attention and, each time I thought about it, I placed one hand over the other and confirmed my love for myself. I could feel my body appreciating my conscious touch and I felt my connection to myself in a non-sexual pleasurable way.

It's a different sensual feeling to touch your body without orgasm as the goal. You can experience your sexuality just by touching your hands together lovingly, stroking your own face as you watch your expression in the mirror, or bathing each body part with the gentle touch of a lover.

The next time you get a massage, make a decision not to fall asleep or talk to the masseuse during the massage. Tune into your body's responses to touch. Notice what part of your body seems to be craving touch. It may not be an obvious part, such as your tense shoulders or sore back.

When you are with a lover, cuddle, hold hands, and dance cheek to cheek in your living room. Sit with your lover's head resting in your lap and gently stroke the hair back from their forehead. Mothers often do this with their children, and it will evoke in your partner the memory of gentle care. Massage each other's hands. Hug each other from behind and touch your faces together for a few moments as you *feel* the hug. Outline each other's faces with your fingers. Place your hands on each other's hearts and connect with the wonder of the heartbeats. Feel life beating inside both of you. Look into each other's eyes with hands still touching hearts and bless the sacredness of the moment. Bless the sacredness of your energies—feminine and masculine in both of you—blending.

Becoming intimate with your sense of touch creates a wider pathway to your sexuality and your essence. Once you know what you enjoy and how you respond, you will be better able to communicate with your partner. Your partner will be excited to participate in sensual foreplay with a greater awareness of you and with great anticipation of the sexual activity to follow.

INNER EXPLORATION

Get in touch with your touch and everything that you touch.

1. Surround yourself with things that feel good to your touch—sensuous silk and satin clothing, thick bath towels warm from the clothes dryer, heated oils, cool powders.

2. Be aware of everything you touch. Feel the velvety touch on your skin of flower petals placed in your bath. Notice how a loofah brush stimulates your body's surface and a hairbrush stimulates your scalp. Feel the leaves of a plant and the life within each leaf. Feel the response of a pet as you gently stroke the top of the animal's head.

3. Hold your own hand. Stroke your face lovingly in the mirror. Caress your ears. Massage your feet. Hug yourself and feel it! Make each touch deliberate and conscious for maximum effect.

4. Notice how you hug people. Do you hug fully and completely, or are you a half-hearted hugger? If you are a half-hearted hugger, ask yourself why.

Is it because you feel too vulnerable? Is it because you don't really feel connected to the touch of another? Are you using the excuse that this is how your family hugged and it's all you know?

5. Ask yourself if the way you hug is the way you want to be hugged. If you are not happy with the way you have been hugging people, you can change it by being present, staying in your heart, and fully feeling the connection when you hug.

~~~~~~~

The Sense of Smell

Smell has the most direct route to our minds. Scent molecules travel directly from the nose to the brain and cause an immediate reaction. Smell can turn us on or turn us away. Smell can cause us to smile in anticipation or in fond remembrance. The smell of a new baby is unforgettable. When we receive flowers, our first response is to smell them, and in that instance we create a memory and attach a feeling to the sender. The smell of roasted chicken may prompt memories of Grandma's house when we were growing up. Fresh-baked pies evoke memories and anticipation of holidays.

When you put on perfume, do you ever notice that you are sensually stimulated by the scent? Do you walk into a room a little bit differently when you are wearing your favorite scent? I am aware that I not only respond to the scent of a man's cologne, but also to my own perfume. I feel more sensual when I am wearing a scent that others, even strangers, call appealing. Consider how you *feel* when you smell the lingering scent of a lover's cologne on your pillow after they have left for work.

One of the first friends I had when I moved to Arizona in 1989 had the most wonderful-smelling home, which inspired me to be conscious of the smells in my own home. Each time I walked into her home, I smelled a combination of "Claire Burkes Original Potpourri Scent," jasmine incense, and fresh flowers. Since she owned a restaurant and was a great cook, the smell of fabulous food was generally entwined as well. The smells alone made me feel good being there. After my first visit to her house, I went home to create the scents that I enjoy for myself. The first thing I notice when I enter my front door now are the smells of orchid potpourris and vanilla and orange candles. When I walk into my bedroom, I enjoy the smell of lavender.

I recall my ex-husband visiting me after many years apart. Getting into my car, he grinned and said, "It smells like you in here." I asked, "What does that smell like?" He responded that it smelled like my makeup and my shampoo. I watched his face brighten as he brought up fond memories of our past. It was a nice moment.

Creating great aromas in your surroundings soothes your soul and the souls of those who come into your environment. After they have gone, you will linger in their minds.

Enhancing your sense of smell and creating an atmosphere of special scents that remind others of you will be an enjoyable experiment. If you have a partner, massage him or her with warm scented oils. Lavender, jasmine, and sandalwood promote a calming experience. Light spice candles for an exotic, seductive scent. Immerse yourself in a scented bath of rose and jasmine before you make love or even when you're home alone. Smell is romantic, heady, healing, and sensual.

Inner Exploration

1. What are your favorite scents? Orange, lavender, spice, rose, gardenia, chocolate, licorice, mint, cinnamon, lemon, lime, rosemary, or musk? Whatever they are, bring them into your home in combinations that complement each other. Refresh or replenish them as often as possible to create a constant, sensual, comforting atmosphere that reminds you of the importance of scent.

2. If you are with a partner, find out what their favorite scents are. When you are together, be sure to create an atmosphere that unites both of your favorite aromas. In addition to the pleasure provided in the present, this facilitates fond remembrance after the experience has passed. Again, keep this practice of scents consistent and imaginative.

~~~~~~~~

The Sense of Hearing

Not long ago, I went to a concert by the sensual singer, Sade. Early in the show, I half-jokingly told my partner that the arena where Sade was performing needed beds not chairs because her music was so sexy, one could hardly wait to get home and make love.

Lovemaking is enhanced by the suggestions of music. Music summons great joy. Dancing to music puts many in a joyful and sensual mood. Listening to different types of music, whether Latin, jazz, soul, or rhythm and blues, often elevates sexuality. Rock and roll from the seventies puts some in a wilder, freer state. New Age music is calming and tribal music erotic. It's fun to become aware of the effects of different types of music on your body, mind, and spirit.

You may notice that if you aren't particularly in the mood for lovemaking, playing certain kinds of music will begin to shift your feelings. Being in the mood or not being in the mood is a state of the mind, not of the body. When we become aware that sound can alter our minds, we have another tool to enhance our enjoyment and that of our partner. When we discover what different sounds do for us, we can use them to produce the effect we desire.

It's not only human-made music that is seductive and brings us joy. It's also the music of the ocean as the waves rush to the shore, or the voice of a babbling brook flowing over and around the stones and rocks along its path. The thrust of a waterfall or the gentle sound of rain makes a delicious backdrop for sensual feelings as well.

And then there is the sound of our voices as we speak ever so lovingly to each other and, equally important, to ourselves. How we speak to ourselves has a great influence on how we speak to our lovers. When we learn to encourage and inspire ourselves verbally and take note of how we respond to our own loving communication, encouraging and inspiring our partners will come more naturally. The sound of one's own loving, nurturing, approving voice is indeed music to our ears.

Take note of the tone of your voice as you interact with others throughout your day. Notice how your tone of voice affects them. Pay attention to the sound of others' voices as they speak to you and notice the effect they have on you.

Listen to the sounds of life, and surround yourself with sounds that lift your spirit whenever you have the opportunity.

When you change the state of your mind by introducing various sounds into your life, you can transcend stress, improve your concentration, induce a feeling of elation and well-being, and stimulate your sexuality.

INNER EXPLORATION

1. Write down the sounds that create a feeling of well-being in you.

2. Write down the sounds that create sensual feelings in you.

3. Devote an entire day this weekend to being surrounded by the sounds that have a positive effect on your body, mind, and spirit. In the course of this day, be sure that the sounds that you choose to be around have the components of your answers to the above questions.

4. Be aware of how your voice sounds to yourself and others throughout this particular day. Speak gently, speak compassionately, speak as you would want to be spoken to.

5. In the evening, be aware of how you feel and write about your day. Notice how you can consciously change your state of mind through sound.

~~~~~~~

The Sense of Sight

Every moment contains a revelation in vision. The sense of sight is perhaps the most profound of the five senses because of its dual nature: outer and inner sight. We look out from our eyes through the filter of our inner selves. What we see in the world is colored by our perceptions, so no two people see the same way, even when they are looking at the same thing.

If we do not use our sight, both inner and outer, to see ourselves as beautiful, grand, and magnificent, we will never experience the width and the breadth of our sexuality nor appropriately experience the sexuality of another.

Our acceptance of the sight of our bodies, as well as how we see ourselves from the inside out, contributes strongly to our sexuality. Author Dennis Prager talks of the "missing tile syndrome." He says, "Look at a ceiling that has every tile except one. What does your eye always focus on? The missing tile, of course." If we focus on what is imperfect, we fail to recognize that which is grand. And all of us, every one of us, are grand. There is no one else like you in the entire world, and that is grand.

Our eyes are organs of stimulation, windows to the soul, and the sense through which we derive visual pleasure. Our sense of sight is stimulated by magnificent landscapes, a dolphin leaping out of a glistening ocean, a monarch butterfly alighting on a vibrant rose, a rainbow, the outline of candlelight on our beloved's face, the unique curve of our lover's lips. Our inner sight is equally key to *seeing*—who we truly are, who our partners truly are. Our inner sight will have us celebrating our partners' uniqueness, and recognizing that they have their own set of wants, needs, and desires. The differences between two people are meant to be celebrated, not regarded as a deterrent. Each of us holds a piece of the Divine in all of our facets, if we could only see that.

Have you noticed how you are physically and emotionally moved even deeper into your feeling of sensuality when dining in the aura of candlelight, or how you are stimulated when making love in front of a seductive fire or dancing under the light of the silvery moon?

Creating an atmosphere that stimulates your sense of sight need not be reserved for the times when you are with your lover. Forming sacred space for yourself by making your surroundings visually appealing stimulates your outer sense of sight, while calming your inner vision.

Make your bedroom look and feel as appealing to you when you enter it alone as it does when you alter the atmosphere to bewitch your beloved. Consciously shaping every room in your home to look and feel appealing is another part of celebrating your glorious self and nourishing your spirit. What your environment looks like is an extension of your soul, an expression of your unique soul print on this earth. When someone enters your home, your surroundings tell that person a great deal about who you are. Similarly, when you enter other people's homes, you gain a greater awareness of who they are.

Notice when people go to the lake or to the ocean how they will pull out a lounge chair and just sit and watch the beauty for hours. They are peacefully stimulated by the tranquility of what they see. Sight (both inner and outer) is another sense that we have to shift our moods. We don't have to wait to go somewhere else to see what makes us feel good or moves us. We can create that no matter where we are. When you become aware of how much influence your sight has on you, you will begin to honor it.

Consider your reaction or first impression at the sight of someone new, or the first impressions people have had of you. How we put ourselves together on the outside has much to do with how we are perceived. Dressing with loving care is another way of expressing our love for ourselves. As an added benefit, people are naturally attracted to what is visually pleasing.

Marianne Williamson told a funny story at one of her lectures. When she was a little girl and traveled with her family, her mother would always tell her to dress comfortably when going on an airplane. Years later, as an adult, she took a plane trip with a girlfriend and was dressed in keeping with her mother's early instructions. Her girlfriend met a great guy on the airplane. Upon exiting the plane, Marianne asked, "Why is it that everyone but me meets men on airplanes?" Her girlfriend's response was, "Look at the way you dress."

As Marianne has said more than once, "Stop waiting until someone comes along to be fabulous. Start practicing being fabulous now and someone will come along!"

That means be glorious and fabulous—inside and out.

INNER EXPLORATION

1. Look around your home. Does it visually stimulate you? If you were to entertain a friend or your beloved, would you do anything differently? If your answer is yes, define it and do it—now, for yourself. No need to wait for guests to arrive.

2. Notice how you put yourself together when you go out. What do you believe will be someone's first impression of you, based on sight?

3. If you are already in a relationship, are you aware that you receive each other differently when you are well put-together? Has either of you or have both of you become a little too comfortable a little too often? Have you stopped creating visual feasts to woo your partner?

4. Using both your inner and outer sight, look in the mirror. What response do you get at the sight of yourself?

~~~~~~~

THE ART OF CONSCIOUS LOVING

If you weren't aware of it before, you know by now that all of our senses are linked to each other for the optimum life experience. Heightening our senses is using everything that God gave us for experiencing life, consciously enjoying our sexuality, and appreciating all parts of ourselves and our partners.

The art of conscious loving comes about when we maximize and explore with our beloved all of our senses in order to enhance our sexual pleasure, and when we strip ourselves down to the unvarnished vulnerability of who we truly are. Then, and only then, will we experience the deepest, most honest level of communion with a partner.

Conscious loving is not about having sex with just anyone; it is about being in a passionate partnership, one that is completely open, honest, and consciously maintained. Conscious loving is cultivating the art of both sexual and nonsexual love as a skillful spiritual practice.

Author Margot Anand wrote, "Sex is at the root of life and to make human sexuality and erotic union a form of worship and meditation is to practice reverence for life, leading us directly through the pleasure of the senses to spiritual liberation."

Our sexuality is a spiritual energy intended to be an expression of love. The goal of conscious loving is to achieve a state of balance between the aspects that characterize the feminine energy and the aspects that characterize the masculine energy, to harmonize yin and yang and swim in a field of unified consciousness. When we achieve this state of balance, we eclipse duality and enter a condition known as bliss. Shakespeare wrote, "And when love speaks, the voice of all the Gods makes heaven drowsy with the harmony."

To love consciously is to know what your needs are, to express them in a loving manner, and to know clearly through communication, not by your thoughts, the needs of your partner. Having a mutual understanding of each other's needs is vital to the journey of our souls. All relationships are based upon the ability to give and take. We will not miss what we give up if the relationship is consciously maintained. Conscious loving calls upon us to "see or saw," depending on the day. It also calls upon us to approach each other not from our fear and self-righteousness, but from our similarities.

There is a term in Latin, *sine qua non,* which literally means 'without which not.' It's used to describe an essential condition or element, an indispensable thing, even an absolute prerequisite. A relationship always entails concessions. Each unique one of us, however, has something that is so important to us that we cannot be in a relationship that doesn't include that element. It's the *sine qua non* of a relationship. Without it, the connection just won't work well for us. Therefore, it's essential for both people in a relationship to express what that one thing is for them.

For example, mine is romance. I cannot be in a relationship with a man who is not romantic. My definition of romance is probably atypical. It's not the ongoing fantasy of trails of rose petals leading to my champagne-filled bath (not that I don't love that). For me, romance is present when someone is aware of what's going on in my life and through his actions honors that. Here's an example.

At work, I'd had a particularly harried week of long days, a lot of expectations, and a few too many commitments. The man in my life at the time had also had an exceptionally busy week, which included business travel. We were both looking forward to a relaxed weekend. On Friday evening, I overheard him on the phone with a friend who was apparently asking if we wanted to get together and go out for dinner. My friend said, "You know, Maureen has had such a hectic week, I think she needs some pampering. I think we'll just stay home and I'm going to cook her dinner." When I heard him say that, I was deeply touched by his awareness of my week, despite his own, and felt grateful to have him in my life. That, for me, was romantic, and went a long way.

Other examples of "must haves" that I have heard from friends and clients are:

"I must be in a relationship where my thoughts are respected."

"I must be in a relationship with someone who doesn't put work before me."

"I must be in a relationship with someone who knows how to play."

"I must be in a relationship with someone who loves animals."

"I must be in a relationship where my feelings are cherished."

"I must be in a relationship with a person who is optimistic about life."

"I must be in a relationship with someone who takes pride in their appearance."

These are just a few examples of people who know what they absolutely must have in a relationship, and are clear about stating it. It's important for each partner in a relationship to identify their *sine qua non*. You can then sit down and share with each other the *one* thing that you each feel must be honored and cherished or the relationship will be in jeopardy. If you do this, you will find that you are much more able to compromise in other areas. When your partner is honoring that one thing that is so important to you and you are doing the same for him, consciously and continually, you will expand and grow together. You will have a shared consciousness of what it means to be in a sacred union. From there, you can ask the next question: What can I do to love you more?

That is conscious loving.

Conscious loving takes relationships and sexuality from the mundane to the mystical. It moves you from rigidity to flexibility, and from the illusion of love to real love. Conscious love provides you with the opportunity to experience vulnerability, openheartedness, courage, and surrender. This kind of love moves the soul forward in its quest for evolution.

If you choose to bring back the vitality of your sexuality and feel deeply your sensuality, do not be cautious when your heart and soul ask you to stop navigating your course. Trust and give in to the blissful surrender for which your heart and soul are yearning. Open wide to let love in.

CHAPTER 5

Soul

Let your life speak.
—an old Quaker saying

Many brilliant words have been used in defining the soul and detailing its role and function in life. Often lost in this flood of words is the vital importance of actualizing the soul's communication and, in so doing, activating our lives.

The journey to bliss requires more than simply understanding what has been written about Balance, Love, Integrity, Sexuality, and **Soul**, the last element of BLISS. It requires us to experience these elements in order for them to have meaning for our lives. Definition alone gives one only an intellectual understanding. Just as there can be no wisdom without knowledge applied, there can be no bliss without action applied.

To experience bliss fully is to bring your life back into *balance*, to open your heart completely to giving and receiving *love*, to live your life purposefully and honorably with *integrity*, to experience with sacredness your *sexuality*, and to have the faith, courage, and ability to surrender to the message of your *soul*.

Simply put, the soul is the Divine Spark of Life that is our essential nature. The soul is the part of ourselves that validates our deepest truths. Stored in the soul is all the information about Who We Are and what we are here to do. The soul is an invisible dimension of experience whose language is love, depth, and reflection.

To understand the varying definitions of the soul is much less important than listening to the message given to you by your soul. If you cannot silence yourself long enough to listen to your soul, you will be unable to live the life that was intended for you, and designed by God and you long before you came here. Can you imagine the ramifications to your spirit?

What if Martin Luther King Jr. hadn't listened to his soul and decided to be an actor? What if Mahatma Gandhi hadn't listened to his soul and became a monk? What if Maya Angelou hadn't listened to her soul and became an attorney? What if Meryl Streep hadn't listened to her soul and became a singer? What if Oprah Winfrey hadn't listened to her soul and became a painter? What if Mother Teresa hadn't listened to her soul and became a housewife?

This doesn't apply only to celebrities and world leaders. Every person on earth has a vital role. Think about your family physician, your favorite florist, your precious pet's veterinarian, the owner of the day care center to whom you entrust your child. What if the thousands of others who have had and will continue to have a positive impact in some way in the lives of others hadn't listened to their souls? What do you believe the impact would be on each of us, and on this planet? What if you're not listening to your soul and have become professionally what your ego or your parents wanted you to be, or what you *thought* would be a good idea to be? What if you have simply settled for the presumed easy way out, but it has turned instead into a grueling life?

If we have settled, rather than listened to the soul's message, then we are not living our lives with integrity. Remember, integrity is when our inner self is in harmony with our outer self. If we're not in integrity, we're out of balance, and if we're out of balance, we can't love well or honor our soul. When any of the five elements are missing, we are unable to experience bliss.

Choosing our professions and activities soulfully is not about seeking prestige (or even simplicity). It *is* about the vivid sense of living with passion that is lost if we don't listen. When we fail to listen to our soul, the message is not delivered and the good we could have done doesn't occur. We don't feel content, our originality has no chance to emerge, and peace does not descend upon our very essence as it does when we receive and act upon the messages from our soul.

If you are not listening to your soul, you are living the wrong life. And you can feel it—just as if you're a size ten and wear a size eight pair of pants, you feel uncomfortable. You're not meant to be wearing the wrong size, just as you're not meant to be living the wrong life. If you don't feel good about your life, more than likely you have failed to heed your soul and have taken a wrong turn, missed a marker, given up, or copped out. If you think your mind can figure a way out of your current circumstances, you are incorrect. If you think that things will change for the better if you just wait, you're incorrect. Your only way out is to start listening to your soul and activating your authentic life—the life you were meant to live, the reason, the purpose behind your whole existence here. Anything other than that is as constricting as wearing the wrong size pants.

Some might respond, "But at this stage of the game, I don't know how to get from where I am to where I think my soul is asking me to go."

I address this issue in detail later in this chapter, but for now, I will simply say: I promise you that if your soul is suggesting that you do something different in your life and it's calling you (or dragging you at this point) in another direction, and if you listen and take action, *everything* that you need will be provided for you to make your way to your soul's call.

INTERPRETING THE LANGUAGE
OF THE SOUL

The soul rarely requests something to which it is easy for our mind and personality to respond. The challenge for many of us comes from our normal way of grasping life. The mind speaks to us literally and gives us answers, reasons, logic, and pros and cons. The mind speaks from a limited perspective. The soul speaks to us in images, the meanings of which are sometimes difficult for the mind to interpret. The soul speaks from an unlimited Source. It offers impressions, insinuations, and desires that often seem illogical or unreasonable to the ego or in relation to our current way of life. The mind and ego are not subtle; they are insistent, persistent, and difficult not to hear. The soul speaks in more subtle tones and abandons typical clarity.

To hear the soul requires a different kind of listening, which I call awareness, to distinguish it from the kind of listening that the mind and ego require. When the soul communicates, it preserves mystery. The mind, on the other hand, thinks a mystery has to be solved and manages to come up with a boisterous answer. Mystery has its own appeal, but to just *be* with mystery is challenging for a society that lives for answers.

When we are aware of what our soul—our authentic life—is saying to us, we live from a deeper place where life is fundamentally mysterious. The mystery gives us the opportunity to experience unique passions and unpredictable dreams that open a point of entry for Life in all of its richness to slip in. A life lived gracefully in the mystery is life expanded and opened to its fullest potential. In this way, we access our ultimate creative selves and find joy in the process of unfolding.

One of my friends asked me if I had outlined this book. My response was, "Oh no, I wanted to see what the book had in store for me!" I knew overall what I was going to write about, but the unfolding was a sublime mystery. Every day of its incarnation was an incredible revelation.

In *Original Self,* Thomas Moore wrote, "To deal with the powerful urges of the deep soul, a poetic attitude rather than a rational one is more effective." For us to interpret the soul, we must learn to interpret differently, watchfully, quietly, with inner eyes and without a rush to judgment. The mind is used to comprehending and evaluating what it hears by applying judgments formed by past experiences it hasn't let go of.

The word 'comprehend' is of Latin origin and consists of the roots *cum*, which means 'with,' and *prehendere*, which means 'to grasp or pick up.' Therefore, to comprehend means to pick something up and be one with it. In order to really comprehend or understand something, we must pick it up and be still with it. Similarly, that's how we learn to comprehend what the soul, in its subtle way, is saying to us: By being aware that there is information coming through and, rather than interpreting it in the way we are accustomed to interpreting information, we are just quietly one with it. When we are one with the information, without judgment, we merge with the energy of it and the translation just is. The process becomes a natural translation of information without mental interference. This leads us to a different mode of comprehension.

Learning a new language takes practice. When we learn how to comprehend information from the soul, we begin to transform our life situations, which have been based primarily on information from the mind.

Listening to the soul becomes easy when we remove from our limited minds all barriers as to what we can or can't do. It comes more naturally when we are able to leave behind all negative thoughts concerning our worthiness and our beliefs in lack and limitation, and surrender to the great Universal Mind. When we do this, we open to having experiences larger and grander than we *thought* we could.

We can learn how to replace our old thoughts and patterns of behavior by incorporating the previous four aspects of BLISS into our lives. What it takes to change our inner and outer landscapes is the creation of a new thought and new pattern of behavior in each moment. With that accomplished, or in the process of accomplishment, the ability to hear the soul speak will be easier and the desire to respond will be even greater.

There is only One Mind, One Intelligence, and each of us is a part of it. That One Mind speaks to us through our individuated souls. Since we are of Spirit and a part of the only Intelligence there is, we are able to draw upon that Intelligence and Power and use it to help carry out the Divine Plan. We are each part of the Divine Plan for this planet to move forward toward enlightenment. We are each a critical player and that is why we each have a soul, through which the Universal Soul speaks to us and lets us know what we are to do for the success of the whole. When you understand that you are part of the whole and not an island where your immediate gratification is of highest importance, you will come to understand with great reverence the complex weavings between above and below in your particular incarnation. Do not underestimate your part in the Plan. Do not distract anybody else from theirs.

If you are a member of a rowing team and are off gardening instead of doing your part, the one you are asked to do, there is a void because a unique strength that only you can offer is missing. Everyone on the team will feel, on some level, that something is missing.

We are here to be team players with unique individual roles.

BEING PART OF THE TEAM

When any one of us follows the call of the soul and lives the life we are meant to lead, we initiate a wave of energy that merges with mass conscious energy. That is the energy of right action and passion, and it is infectious. That energy has the ability to change the landscape of this planet. Part of living on this planet is to accept our positions as Spirits having a human experience and join the team of mankind to serve the greater good of all concerned. This is not merely making charitable contributions a couple of times a year or volunteering for a charity on a semi-regular basis. It means living your soul's request, your authentic life—*daily*. It means if your soul is asking you to be a comedienne, a massage therapist, or a gardener, be it. If your soul is asking, there is a reason.

We make the mistake of believing that one person can't make a difference. We don't deeply understand that in order to find our bliss and have the planet that we are residing on experience her bliss, we must become aware and take right action with the only thing that is forever—the soul. Your soul is the only thing you brought with you into this life from a previous time, and it will be the only thing you take with you for future time, which suggests it must be quite important. It is not to be taken lightly and not to be ignored. It is your job to become aware of and intimately involved with your soul. Your soul needs to be heard.

When you are doing what your ego thinks you ought to be doing or following the lead of the mind—doing anything that you know deep down does not feed your Spirit—you are on the dance floor by yourself.

Our individual choice of whether or not to live out our soul's calling affects the entire human race. We are energetic beings feeding off the energy of every living thing around us. As we well know, what we eat has everything to do with how our body will operate and the level of energy available to us. What we do with our lives has everything to do with the life force of our individual souls and the life force of our planet.

There is no separation.

INNER EXPLORATION

1. Remove yourself from any distractions—television, stereo, light, children, conversation, the future, or the past. Have your journal handy. Take seven deep breaths. Put forth the intention that this time of silence will be dedicated to listening to your life, your soul, talking to you.

2. Make the commitment not to allow your thoughts, judgments, or rationalizations to interfere with this communication with your soul.

3. Become aware. Listen to your soul. Don't respond. Listen to your soul. Be still. Be silent. Listen to your soul.

4. What do you hear when the mind is quiet and you relinquish your fear? Don't expect your soul to give you your entire life message in one sitting. It won't, but what it will do is give you information you need now. Each time you still yourself, it will give you more.

5. What has your soul just conveyed to you? Write it down in your journal. Be with it.

6. Now, what will you do with this information?

HEEDING THE SOUL'S MESSAGE

> There is a price and a prize in heeding the message
> of the soul.
>
> The price: your life as you have known it will never
> be the same.
>
> The prize: your life as you have known it will never
> be the same.

To hear your soul's message is not enough. Once heard,
you must act upon it. You can pretend that you didn't hear
it, but you will always be pricked by the knowingness that
you did. Until you take action, you will be aware that something is missing. If you don't take action, you will become
more unsettled about your life than ever before, because your
soul has given you pertinent information in regard to your
journey. Not listening to the message as it is revealed will
put you in jeopardy of missing the point of your life. Wouldn't
it be tragic to live seventy or eighty years on this planet and
miss the point of your life? Many do.

Your soul won't give you the entire message at one time.
If it did, it would overwhelm you from the limited perspective of the mind or you might decipher the message incorrectly. Instead, the mystery will lure you to seek more. It
will summon an unfamiliar longing in you. It will request
that you employ every aspect of the deepest meaning of faith,
courage, and surrender so you can live in a manner that you
have never dreamt of, or perhaps you have, but it remains a
dream. You will have the opportunity to live your
dream...awakened.

When we still the mind, that which is natural and joyful continues to prevail. What ceases is what Edward Carpenter describes as "that joyless quest," which is inevitable for the mind as it perpetually raises questions and doubts. Then, continues Carpenter, "There comes to man a sense of absolute repose, a consciousness of immense and universal power, such as completely transforms the world for him."

FAITH

Faith is the first thing required once any part of the soul's message has been revealed.

In the beginning, faith is not a comfortable or automatic response for us when listening to the subtleties of the soul's message. It has become, by virtue of habit, quite comfortable trusting the "logic" of the mind. By nature, our soul is the Original Source, and it would only make sense to trust it despite the mind's aversion to doing so. Now we are asked to untangle the wire and plug back into the Original Source to make a clear connection. We are accustomed to having faith in our thoughts, and now we're implored to use our faith in the opposite direction. Faith is belief in what we don't see or hear in the usual manner but know in the bowels of our being to be right.

When you get a message from the soul, asking others' opinions about it operates against faith. Opinions are like front doors; everybody has one. It has been my repeated experience that when I receive guidance from my soul and ask others for their opinion of my message, the response typically argues against my soul's message and confuses me.

But that's not surprising. What would somebody else's opinion have to do with the message of my soul or your soul? Perhaps one out of a hundred opinions might be in harmony with my message or your message, but why waste precious energy discerning which of the hundred is correct? Faith does not have to ask anybody else's opinion.

Some of us have faith in negatives. For example, we might be sure that "it's only a matter of time before the other shoe will drop," or "we've just been lucky *this* time." We manage to have faith that something bad will happen because things have been going too smoothly, or that we'll probably get the flu because everyone around us is sick. We have mastered negative faith quite brilliantly. Negative faith is a product of the mind's belief system. Now the soul is asking us to have positive faith, which springs from the soul. How do we do that? We break the old habit of negative faith.

Breaking the Habit of Negative Faith

Breaking the habit of negative faith is no more or less difficult than breaking the habit of smoking, drinking, eating sugar, biting our nails, or grinding our teeth. Again, it takes intention, commitment, diligence, and vigilance. You must watch yourself closely and witness when you slip back into the old familiar pattern of negative thinking, or negative faith. Don't let a day go by in which you are unaware of yourself and how you operate. Faith requires you to become the conscious watcher of your own life in order to anchor in positive faith. Judgment is not required here, simply awareness.

Something I have found helpful in becoming the conscious observer of myself is this: the moment I wake up in the morning,

I silently observe the interior landscape of my body and mind. I lie in bed and take a morning inventory. Have I woken up calm, or am I already steeling myself in anticipation of the day ahead? Are my thoughts racing ahead of the present moment, or am I feeling even and balanced? Am I edgy because I didn't sleep well last night, or am I anxious because I went to bed with unresolved issues? I don't judge, I just observe.

During my observation, I make adjustments. If I'm feeling out of balance, I note what part of me is idling a little too fast. I take a deep breath, and I ask that part to please come into balance and harmony with all my other parts. I am well aware that if I wake up uncomfortable with what's going on in any part of me, I will have to be even more aware of my thoughts and actions throughout the day. If I am not aware, there is a good chance that I will say negative things to myself and others, and I may well take a negative approach to almost anything that comes up during the day.

After my morning inventory, I say the morning prayer from Marianne Williamson's prayer book, Illuminata. This particular prayer brings me back to the awareness that this is a new day and a new opportunity with all things possible. It brings me back to positive faith. I feel good invoking this prayer and tend to linger a while longer with the Divine before I put my feet on the floor.

Before I get out of bed, I also ask God to bless everything that I speak, think, say, and do, so that I may move through the day with Grace. I begin my day with an open heart and an open mind as often as "humanly" possible. I perch my little Maureen on the shoulder of big Maureen so there is an awareness of myself, my thoughts, my patterns, and my habits as I move through the day.

Since I am a morning person, I have the tendency to want to wake up and get going quickly. But I have noticed that a fast approach tires me out earlier in the day and provides an opportunity for negativity to creep in when I'm not paying attention. When we're tired, lonely, or hungry, negative thoughts find their way inside. When I came to this awareness, I began to recreate and balance more evenly the way I typically go about my day. I tried different things at different times to see what might feel best, instead of assuming that the schedule I set up for myself long ago was still serving me. I changed patterns created over decades and became more flexible with my life. I began to ask my body what it needed each day, and I listened when it wanted pancakes with a protein drink for breakfast instead of eggs. I noted when it asked to take a walk instead of going to the gym on a particular day. I paid attention when it signaled to me that it needed to sit on the porch for a while and feel the breeze, even though my mind wanted to write another few pages.

Before going to sleep at night, I take another inventory. What occurred in my day? Did old thought forms find their way in and have me doubting myself or my life? I check to see if I'm feeling anxious about anything that I said or did. Did I operate in integrity and, if not, what was the fear that caused my behavior? I write it down. I observe what I wrote. I then write down at least five things for which I was grateful in my day. This reminds me of the good in my life. I thank God for all of my blessings and all of my awareness. I read the evening prayer from Illuminata. I forgive myself my shortcomings of the day. I bless the people on whom I took my feelings out. When I have messed up miserably, in spite of my awareness, I make myself laugh by remembering a saying of an old friend of mine. He said, "Give yourself an A+ for being human and get over it!" I have faith that tomorrow will resurrect that which may have fallen today.

Once the habit of negative faith is broken, it need never plague you again. It will test you from time to time, like any old habit does, to see if you're still committed to your highest intention. At some point, you may even find your old habit amusing and know what's happening the moment it kicks in. With an awareness of how wonderfully your new habit of positive faith is working for you, you will find the old habit absurd.

The beauty of having positive faith rather than negative faith is that it requires much less thinking. When the mind devises a plan, we think altogether too much about too many things. The potentials, the hazards, the what ifs, the what abouts, the should I, the what would so and so do if they were in my shoes, and on and on, ad nauseam. The answers we come up with to carry out the mind's current plan are based on past experiences. We typically author our future by our experience of the past. Keep in mind that whatever you decide is what you will manifest in your outer world. Whatever you have faith in, negative or otherwise, is precisely what you will bring into your life.

When the soul communicates its message, we have the opportunity of not thinking and instead learning to trust, to have faith, because the message from the soul is coming directly from the Divine. Asking all of the foolish questions is an exercise in futility because the answers are already in place. If you have faith in the message and the Messenger, you won't have to devise a plan. The message carries the plan. When the ego mind devises the plan, its machinations create all kinds of opportunities for chaos. The soul *has* the plan and the message is unified in purpose. Having faith in the message of the soul is thought control. Imagine!

When positive faith nests in our spirit, we will attain, as it says in the Bible, "the peace that passeth all understanding."

Having faith in the message of the soul does not mean that it will be a cakewalk from that point forward. Our past conditioning will intrude at times, and faith has its own conditioning requirements. Faith, when all is said and done, is persistence.

Calvin Coolidge said, "Nothing in the world can take the place of persistence. Talent will not; nothing is more common than unsuccessful men with talent. Genius will not; unrewarded genius is almost a proverb. Education will not; the world is full of educated failures. Persistence and determination alone are omnipotent."

Like water that, drop by drop, wears down a rock, faith held *in spite of what appears to be* will assure that you will arrive safely in harbor no matter how rough the waters seem to be. Your faith is your measure of trust in the message of the soul.

FAITH AND THE SOUL

Faith is trust. It is not hope. It is a knowing. Hope is frail and holds a dim light that flickers on and off. It has aspects of optimism but, in truth, a hopeful attitude is a pessimistic attitude looking at things optimistically. To have hope in the message of the soul is no more than a querulous wish for something good to happen. Hope carries itself hunched over in a weak attempt to better our lives. It is for this reason that hopeful people's lives rarely change. Hope is wishing, and if we are wishing for something to be, then some part of us believes it will *not* be. Remember, intention, if not held unwaveringly as true and already experienced as a positive outcome in our hearts, has no "hope" of happening. It cannot come to fruition.

Faith hears the gentle guidance of the soul and, even though the message is somewhat foreign to the current life situation, there is a knowingness and acceptance of what is being transmitted. Faith is believing in the message whether or not we understand how exactly it will work itself out. Faith bathes all things in radiant illumination.

In chapter four, I spoke of how important it is to heighten our five senses—taste, smell, touch, hearing, and sight—in order to experience our sexuality fully. In this chapter, we go beyond these five senses to our multidimensional senses in order to have faith in the message of the soul.

The soul does not speak to us through the pathways to which we are accustomed. Most of us are familiar with and accept that we have a sixth sense—our intuition. We are able to speak of it fairly easily and it is generally a respected sense. Most of us have experienced our sixth sense and have acted on its information from time to time with great results. That gives us the opportunity to know that there are other aspects of ourselves in motion that we can't see, yet we know they work if we trust them. We have also witnessed the outcome when we don't trust our intuition. In these instances, we often kick ourselves for not listening to our sixth sense when we knew we were being told to do something different.

Our sixth sense, along with numerous other senses, which we may or may not be tapping into at the moment, operates on the intangible planes of human existence. In other words, these senses, or forces, are operating whether or not we see them. It is imperative to have faith that they are there, in the same manner that we have faith that our sixth sense is there, even though it's not tangible to us in the way our other senses are. If humankind did not believe there were other things in motion beyond what is visible, no one would utter a single prayer. No one would make a silent wish behind closed eyes before blowing out birthday candles. No one would acknowledge a stirring inside, for what could be stirring when everything is known? There would be no light-bulb moments. Epiphany would be an eight-letter word without definition.

Having faith in something unseen is feeling its insistence and believing that something that we have not yet experienced is possible. This means we are willing to be open and willing to participate in the potential of what isn't seen. We allow what didn't tangibly exist for us before to come into existence. For most people, faith arrives after something is demonstrated. When listening to the message of the soul, faith must precede the demonstration.

Faith is not easily come by when life has been riddled with disappointment. But the life that was is not the life that will be, unless we drag our old baggage along with us. Some fortunate people hear their souls speak to them at a very early age and are beneficiaries of supportive parents, who teach them to be less afraid of rising to the occasion. For these people, faith arises naturally, and they distinctly feel God's blessing. Others of us don't hear the call of our soul until later, and some are still refusing to listen.

For those of us who heard later, it was necessary for our soul's growth, for whatever reason, to experience emptiness, meaninglessness, and disillusionment about life and love. All of that brought us to a hunger and a yearning for our true selves. Yes, it made faith a little harder to find, but God blesses us. Those who refuse to listen to the call of their souls may die with the music still in them. God blesses them, too. Whether sooner or later, we have all been given the Divine birthright to receive the message that our soul has for us about our life, and to have Divine support and assistance in acting on it.

The message coming forth from your soul is your direct link to God, the Higher Power, All That Is. When you listen and activate your life accordingly, a clarity and resolve will burst forth in you, and lift you to a level that in the past you could have only hoped for. When your soul speaks to you, you have the opportunity to accept or reject the message. Whatever you accept, have full faith in, know to be true, and co-create with will be yours. What you reject, you will never know.

INNER EXPLORATION

1. In your journal, enter headings for two categories: What I Have Faith In, and What I Don't Have Faith In. Make a list under each category as to what you have faith in and what you don't have faith in concerning life in general.

2. Look at your list under the second heading. Are you aware that what you don't have faith in is exactly what is missing from your life right now?

3. Look at your list under the first heading. Are the items that you listed things in which you have great faith, or are some of them things you hope for? If they are hopes, move them to a third category called "What I Hope For."

4. Read your lists again. Are you aware that the things that you hope for are also exactly what is missing in your life? Are you aware that the things you have faith in *are* in your life?

5. The second and third lists are records of what your mind is preventing from being in your life in a positive way. Write down your rationales for why you don't have faith in the items on the second list and why you believe your hopes have not turned into positive manifestations.

6. Before you answer this question, read your list of rationales from the previous question again. Now, do you really deep down inside buy into these rationales?

7. Be aware that all of the things you listed under the categories of What I Don't Have Faith In and What I Hope For are nothing more than a sea of potential realities being blocked by an old belief system.

~~~~~~

In my backyard, deer meander through on their daily hikes. They are fascinating to observe. Every few minutes they stop what they are doing, lift their heads, listen, and watch. They have a fine-tuned awareness that is in harmony with everything around them. We as humans have the potential for even higher awareness because of our unique minds. If we slow down and use our minds in tune with the message of the soul, which is already in tune with All That Is, ultimately there will only be one list that will replace all others: What I Know For Sure.

COURAGE

Courage is having the guts to go from *hearing* the message to *doing* something about it. Author Henry Miller wrote, "I believe it absolutely. I know it from my own experience. All growth is a leap in the dark. A spontaneous, unpremeditated act without benefit of experience."

When your soul speaks to you and calls you to your life, all of your previous fears of failure, fears of success, judgments, excuses, guilt, blame, insecurities, and rationales must be abandoned in order to go from the hearing of the message to the activation of the message. The call encourages us to delete our distorted perspective of life and tune in our awareness to life as it really is—from the perspective of the soul. The soul will not give us a message that cannot be manifested.

Having courage allows us to meet ourselves in a new way. I believe that courage is the process of recovering our Divine identity, and that is perhaps why the messages of the soul are at times daunting and demanding. Were the messages simple, they wouldn't have the impact needed to get our attention and afford us the opportunity to see past the illusion of who we think we are, or what we believe we can't do. The message of the soul may seem to be a burden too great to bear, but it is not. All that we need to bring the message of the soul to fruition was given to us long before the message was delivered.

Having the courage to want to know what your soul is asking of you will have you teetering for a moment between excitement and fear. The excitement comes from a belief that there is something for you to do with your life that may release you from the throes of mere survival. The fear comes from the lack of belief that you can do it, or the belief that your outer circumstances are not conducive to you doing it. When fear manages to become the predominant energy, courage becomes a shrinking violet.

It's not realistic to try to rip fear out of you or to deny its existence, however. I have had many clients vehemently deny that they were in fear about one thing or another. It was their vehemence in defending their fort that led us both to know that fear was present. It's okay to be fearful. The only one who views it as not okay is you. What's not okay is to ignore or deny fear. It's a part of you; to deny it is to deny part of yourself.

The energy of fear is a feeling and can be balanced with the energy of mindfulness as its chaperone. Fear and mindfulness coexist and come from the same place inside you. When fear seems to be taking up the majority of space in your house, invite mindfulness, which is your love for yourself, to step in and cradle the fear. Ask the fear what it has to say to you. Be as tender with your fear as you would be with a baby. The fear is crying for attention and, like a baby, it can be calmed down. A crying baby will respond to a nurturing energy. If you are not present with your crying baby because your mind is racing to other things, the baby will feel scattered, too, and won't be able to stop crying. If you are fully present, openhearted, with your breath calm and your words tender, the baby will calm down. So it is with your fear, when the voice of mindfulness, your love for yourself, comes in to "rock the baby."

As with a crying baby, you need to observe your fear to discover the source of the discomfort and suffering. If you treat your fear as you would a baby, you will have the opportunity to see what is at its root. You can then do whatever is necessary to alleviate the discomfort. *Whatever is necessary.* It takes courage to love your fears through their storms and to be responsible for changing any of your life circumstances that are keeping you from activating the message of your soul.

The Courageous Choice

You are only a choice away from living your life the way you were intended to from the beginning. You can choose to remain fearful and full of excuses, or you can choose to be courageous, heed the message of the soul, and allow your mind to turn toward your heart. Your heart is Pure Awareness. In this very moment, as you read this paragraph, you can choose to become responsible for everything you do and every choice that you make. If you want to be happy, all that is asked of you is to make a choice *toward* happiness and not perpetuate the continuation of unhappiness.

Why are our lives the way they are? It's due to the choices that we made, up until this very moment, based on our thoughts, conclusions, and judgments. In every moment of every day, we are making choices, from the moment we awake to the moment of sleep. We choose our brand of toothpaste, we choose the food we eat, we choose to bathe or shower, we choose the clothes we will wear for the day. We choose our attitudes. We choose to be afraid, excited, selfish, or selfless. We choose to call something good or bad, desirable or undesirable. We make choices regarding our jobs and our children. We choose friends and people we are going to let into our lives—or not. Our lives are our choice.

We frequently make our choices in a cavalier manner, failing to understand the magnitude of every choice we make.

People who make a conscious choice to listen to the soul (and it has a message for you regarding every choice you are called upon to make) will always hear it. Those who don't…won't. There are those who say they are torn between this and that. They proclaim that a part of them wants one thing and another part wants something else. There may indeed be parts of you that are talking, but there is only one of you listening. It's up to you to discern the difference between the contradictory impulses of the self and a true message from the soul. You get to choose to doubt whether you can actually be happy, or choose to experience happiness.

To better understand which is the accurate voice speaking to you, in order to make the best choice, notice—that is, become fully aware of—every choice you make. Start with the simple things. How does what you decided to wear today make you feel? How does the breakfast you chose to eat make your body feel? How does the music you decided to listen to in the car make you feel? Starting with an awareness of how you feel about the choices you have made concerning the simpler things in your life will make you more aware of the impact of your choices.

Now consider how you feel about your choice of occupation; your choice of partner, if you are in a relationship; your choice of friends. How do you feel about how you chose to treat people today? How do you feel about how you have chosen to live your life? If you feel divided about your choices, what choices would you change to experience happiness? Know that on some level you have chosen any pain, even physical pain, that you are feeling in the moment.

In the exact moment that I am writing this paragraph, an ice-cream truck is playing its old-fashioned tune over and over again as it makes its way up and down the street. I am very focused on what I'm writing. I can choose to have this music annoy me, or I can enjoy it for its lighthearted-ness and the memories it evokes of days gone by when I would run out to the curb and get a Good Humor Bar. I notice that I immediately choose the latter, and the thought comes to me that tomorrow at this time I will go out to the curb and get an ice-cream bar, something I haven't done in many years. I like the way I feel about my choice.

It takes courage to make choices that soothe our soul and put an end to playing the victim of life. The victim role is no more than old habit. When we have the courage to live an enlightened life, the life that our soul invites us to live, we can no longer hold onto the excuse that we need more time to heal the wounds of the past. More time isn't going to heal them. Your soul-aligned choices will do the healing. And it isn't necessary to get everything in your life a certain way before you give yourself permission to get on with your adventure. If your soul is sending a message now, then now is the time to begin your response. I am not suggesting that you just dump your old life. I am suggesting that you begin to make tracks *daily* to heed the call. Everything else will follow in Divine right order.

Where Courage Leads

There is nothing in this world more liberating than be-ing (and acting) courageous! There is nothing that anchors within you a feeling of self-worth more than being coura-geous. Moving past the fears and into the excitement of the soul's message will lead you to synchronicities about which writers are moved to write and musicians are inspired to sing.

Courage takes you from onions to pearls and sweeps you up in a flow of coincidences that will give you pause. Courage takes you from what you want to what you have in the blink of an eye. You may change jobs, change homes, change relationships, and change your mind. You will be on a mission—your soul mission. You will come to love yourself for your courage and know that love is who you are. It is only by the power of love for self that one can find the courage needed to heed the call of the soul. Jesus taught that only by the power of love can the vital connections be made and the condition of oneness be achieved.

The greatest setback in our lives has been due to the years spent making the wrong connections. The only connections that were or ever will be necessary are our connections with God, Life, and our true natures.

It takes great courage to resist being sucked into the flow *outside* us. It takes great courage to go with the flow *inside* us, to take responsibility for our lives in spite of what seems to be every eye watching and judging us. Know that your courage will be supported.

Once you have decided to activate your life, it will take great courage not to give up five minutes before the miracle happens. The discovery of the message does not skyrocket you from one level of life to another. You will encounter a series of steep inclines and flatlands, followed by twists and turns you would never expect. Approaching the journey with faith and courage is key. Your life mission will not belong to the collective reality with its many limited attitudes.

There are many people who are not participating in their inner journey. Life for them will continue to be a series of dramas they will continue to cast with players much like themselves. The circumstances of their lives are all they have.

Their focus will remain on outer consciousness. They may judge you as having gone off the deep end or insist you are making it all up. It takes courage not to pay attention to their ramblings. It takes courage to trust the message of your soul, and to hold steady to what you are hearing and feeling as you allow the soul to continue to speak to you. If you have the courage to remain open, you will become accustomed to its Voice and waken each day looking forward to its spoken Word.

INNER EXPLORATION

Courage is having the face of a cat and seeing a lion when you look in the mirror.

1. Removed from all distractions, look at yourself in the mirror. Look deeply inside yourself, beyond the obvious, and connect to your courage. Be still and be with your courage. Do not confuse courage—an aspect of your heart—with drive, anger, or ambition, which are aspects of the mind.

2. Become friendly with your courage.

   (a) Ask your courage what it wants of you. Write down all of the answers.

   (b) Write down the first step that you will take today to honor the courageous part of you, to do what your courage asks of you. Once you have accomplished this step, write down how you feel about the choice you made in taking it. Be with that feeling and allow yourself to feel it fully. Don't take it lightly.

(c) Write down the second step that you will take to honor the courageous part of yourself. Once you have accomplished it, write down how you feel about the choice you made in taking it. Be with that feeling and allow yourself to feel it fully. Don't skim past it.

(d) Continue on with steps of courage, one step at a time, one day at a time.

3. Read the following meditation and bring it deep within yourself. Let the words soften the edges of your mind and take up residency in the center of your heart.

I no longer confuse what I seem to be with Who I Really Am. I still my mind and greet my courage. Here in my solitude I am not burdened by thoughts of the past. I have no fear of the future. I listen to the Voice of my soul inside me and I allow it to guide me to my life. I awaken to the sound of my life and feel my well-being as I place myself in the hands of the One Spirit, God. The Consciousness that brought my Spirit here is the Consciousness that will guide me through my life—safely. My path is illuminated with pure white light as I take my first step toward my authentic life.

Every question I have is met with an answer when I still my mind to listen. I trust in the message of my soul and my way is made clear. This day is the birth mother of tomorrow and I create my tomorrows by the choices I make today. I know that I am fulfilling the dream that was always meant for me as I take each step of my life forward with love and with courage.

I bind myself to positive faith and allow the Power for good to surge around and through me. I charge myself with radiant I Am light, and embrace all Power given to me from above and below. My courage dispels the limits and inhibitions of my past. I will live each day from this moment on in accordance with the message from my soul and be lifted into the future of myself. I am indeed blessed. And so it is.

~~~~~~~

SURRENDER

There was a period in my adult life when I honestly believed I was the reincarnation of Job, the man who lived in ancient Israel and whose story is told in the Bible. Job's life was suddenly and repeatedly turned inside out by a plague of what seemed to Job to be other than human trials and tribulations. Indeed, God was testing his faith. In the end, Job passed the test and God restored Job's life to him.

Everything that could possibly go wrong in my life went wrong. In the space of a year, I lost nearly everything—money, business, health, even friendships. I felt ripped off, turned upon, burnt, neglected, and abused by God. It seemed that only a force as strong as God could have brought such destruction into my life. If

I'd had children, as Job did, I believed God would have taken them from me. Job's health failed; my health failed. Job lost all of his money; I lost all of mine. Job felt he was being punished; I was sure I was being punished. Job thought he was losing his mind; I thought I was losing my mind. Job tried to interpret his hardship as some lesson he needed to learn; I spent my days trying to figure out what in the hell I needed to learn. Job tried penance and supplication to God; I did the same. Job sought people who could give him advice and help him through his misery, but nothing changed. I did the same, and nothing changed.

I screamed at God when the pain wouldn't stop. I covered every square inch of my brain to figure a way out, behind God's back. I sank deeper into the pain, deeper into the confusion. I stayed in my pajamas, huddled in a corner of my sofa. I became listless and solitary.

Two of my friends refused to give up on me. Just as I was sure I was about to lose my home, one of my "angels in the flesh," my soul sister Linda (who had tried in every way possible, like Job's friends, to give me spiritual insight) began to get through to me. She said, "Maureen, you don't have to lose your home, you just have to be willing to."

I replied angrily, "I am not willing to lose my home, I have lost enough!"

"It doesn't mean you will lose your home," she said, "but you have to be willing to. You have to surrender, Maureen. You must realize by now that you're fighting a losing battle. It's time to give up the fight. You have been fighting your entire life."

"Well, I'm not willing to lose my home," I said. "This is the only place I get any peace and I'm not going to live in somebody's spare room. Now please go and leave me alone."

She left and the war continued. Three days later, after a sedative-induced sleep, I dragged myself out of bed, threw myself on the floor in my living room, and surrendered. I told the God I still wasn't sure of (but who seemed my only hope), "Go ahead, take my home, take anything you want."

I sincerely meant it. I already felt homeless on this earth, so what difference did it make? The surrender was a lot easier than the struggle had been. It dawned on me that I was giving up the fight for a life I was not meant to have. I made a commitment right there on the spot that I refused to fight with my life anymore. My life would have to come and get me.

Within one week of my surrender, I received a phone call that truly came out of nowhere and turned into a $60,000 piece of business I had never anticipated. Within another week, I received a phone call asking me to appear on a national television talk show as its relationship expert. My life as it was meant to be finally began. It was then that I began to let my soul lead and felt myself rise to meet God on a very different playing field.

Job's story illustrates how our lives can be restored once we surrender our judgments and carryings-on about our hardships. Once Job accepted the good and the difficult of his life and relinquished his search for reasons to explain his twist of fate, the vastness and grandeur of the Universe took over.

Carl Jung expounded on the value of facing adversity: "The unconscious always tries to produce an impossible situation to force the individual to bring out his very best. Otherwise one stops short of one's best, one is not complete, one does not realize oneself. What is needed is an impossible situation where one has to renounce one's own will and one's own wit and do nothing but wait and trust to the impersonal power of growth and development. When you are against a wall, be still and put down roots like a tree, until clarity comes from deeper sources to see over the wall."

What I came to know about surrender is that if you only surrender a portion of what is causing your obstacles, you've aborted the process before it's even begun. Surrendering ninety-eight percent is like surrendering nothing. There must be a complete and total surrender in order for the lights of your life to be turned back on.

INNER EXPLORATION

1. Observe your life in its entirety—your inner and outer world. What parts of your life are you struggling with right now?

2. Are the parts of your life you are struggling with also parts of your life you are fighting to keep?

3. Write down the explanations for why you are willing to fight to keep alive any part of your life with which you are struggling.

4. Do you truly believe your explanations, deep in your soul, or are these explanations that your ego or defense mechanism is spitting out?

5. What obsolete belief system is still running your life and causing you to hold onto something that is not working for you?

6. Be rigorously honest with yourself in regard to this question. What is your payoff for hanging on to the struggle? (There is always a payoff.)

For instance, does it bring you attention you think you need? Do you get to kick back and not have to start over? Is something better than nothing? Is it for what you consider security? Is it for the money? Is it because you don't want to be alone? Is it for the prestige? Is it to be accepted?

7. Observe your answers to the above questions for a few moments without judging or defending them. Just observe.

8. Are you aware of the impact that your life as it is now is having on your spirit?

9. What are you willing to surrender—to give up—in order that your soul has room to breathe and communicate with you? Once you have made your commitment to surrender what you know isn't serving your soul, you must honor your intention. You may find yourself physically taking an action toward or away from something, or you may find yourself withdrawing your thoughts from something that doesn't need your help to work itself out.

~~~~~~~

SURRENDERING TO THE UNKNOWN

Our soul grows more by loss than by gain. When we lose the need to know, we gain clarity. When we lose the need to come up with a game plan, the plan shows itself.

When we give up the need to reinvent ourselves, we are miraculously reinvented. When a door closes, a window opens—always. When we lose the mental grip we have on life and relinquish the need for a five-year plan, the soul has room to extend its message and we give ourselves the space to receive and respond to it.

When you answered the questions in the Inner Exploration above, did you notice your ego kick into gear and begin to defend and justify your responses? That's what the ego does. It justifies, defends, and interferes. The arrogant ego lacks humility, a virtue necessary for us to expand. When we drop the need to defend our choices, we begin to surrender the ego. The ego occupies a great deal of space and believes it knows it all. It leaves little space for what we don't know. Acknowledging what we don't know creates infinite room for the unknown, which frees us from all limitation. The ego is incapable of assisting us in returning to this authentic life. With its arrogance of all-knowingness, it keeps the unknown away.

The message of the soul comes from the unknown, and its goal is our liberation. The statement "I know nothing" gives birth to all that is possible. Only in the surrendering of all that we *think* we know will we come to enlightenment, the profound depth of our Self that abides in a state that relishes the unknown.

The ego never has a true-life experience because it already believes it knows everything about any experience it has. How many times have you made the comment or heard the remark, "I already know what's going to happen," or "I already know what that's all about," or "No big surprise, I told you so." Although I didn't used to be this way, I have come to enjoy observing my belief system at work and watching it be blown to bits when the outcome of a situation is not what I expected. Rather than being embarrassed by that any longer, I am grateful to watch another piece of the illusion slip away, and I surrender it gladly. It's quite liberating when you no longer have to waste energy on being perfect or right, and life lived in that way is magnificent. Surrendering frees you to simply have an experience, be with the experience, and let the outcome unfold.

I am not suggesting for a moment that surrendering is easy in the beginning. For that matter, I'm not certain that it is ever easy—unless we decide it is. We are accustomed to trying to control life with our thoughts and our ego, which is generally in charge of our self-identity. It may feel unstable to rely upon a seemingly unsubstantiated conviction.

Gandhi said, "Our existence as embodied beings is purely momentary; what are a hundred years in eternity? But if we shatter the chains of egotism, and melt into the ocean of humanity, we share its dignity. To feel that we are something is to set up a barrier between God and ourselves; to cease feeling that we are something is to become one with God."

It takes deep love for ourselves and all of creation to surrender to our soul. It takes faith in ourselves to give up what we *thought* we would be when we were enslaved by the mind. We have not been taught to focus our love on ourselves, and we have not been taught that the relationship we have with ourselves creates the relationship we have with all of creation. Having a healthy relationship with one's very essence is an art. We have all given up parts of ourselves to encourage someone else's love. But now, all that we have done to demonstrate our love to someone else must be turned inward. Surrendering is intuitively, not egotistically, coming to know the needs of our body, mind, and spirit so well that we happily give up that which is no longer working for us and accept that which is.

Coming into the state of surrender does not offer immediate gratification. This is a natural process that unfolds at its own pace. If you're only looking for the end result, you will miss the miraculous process. The miracle will be the opportunities, circumstances, and shifts in perception that will magically appear in your life to carry you to wherever or whatever your soul is requesting. Witnessing the re-creation of your life is the miracle. Living life apart from reaction and resistance is a miracle. The opportunity to focus on one thing at a time and not fifty things at a time is a miracle. Not projecting yourself into the future and having that be okay is a miracle. Not having the past haunt you any longer is a miracle. Dissolving lifelong intrusive patterns of the mind is a miracle. No longer struggling to change something not meant to be changed, or easily changing something whose time has come, is a miracle.

Surrender is a powerful transformer and not intended for the meek. It is a high-wire act without benefit of a net. It will shatter the bones of your ego and blow all of your senses wide open. Without faith and courage, surrender and its miracles can never come to pass, and bliss will remain an enigma.

When you begin the process of surrender, all that has been suggested in this book will become reality. Surrender elevates you to a higher vibrational frequency and provides you with opportunities that a vast majority of the Earth's population do not experience. Surrender takes you from mental energy to Spiritual energy, a state in which there is no end to possibility. In *Embracing Heaven and Earth*, Andrew Cohen described surrender as "the most powerful shift of energy and attention that can occur within human con-sciousness, other than the falling away of the physical form."

Surrender extinguishes pain and suffering and returns you to a natural state free from the outer world's tension. Surrender signals to Spirit that all has been made ready for your freedom and the soul has a clear path by which to com-municate. When you surrender, you will find the life that you have been longing for has been lying dormant just be-neath your current life situation.

In the beginning of this book, I shared with you a piece of my early history, much of which was riddled with pain, disappointment, and grief. Still, it was a blessing. Had my life not unfolded in the manner in which it did, I could not have experienced my true relationship to Life and I would have felt fraudulent writing this book. I have scattered pieces of my story throughout the book, so you can see where I started from and know that what I've written about my own transformation describes what is equally possible for you.

Prior to writing this last chapter on soul, my soul spoke to me with a daunting request that required surrendering on a whole new level. Little did I know then that rising to the occasion would not only give me what it would take to write this final chapter from experience and with all my heart, but also would lead me to a deeper love for myself and an experience of bliss beyond my previous awareness. I hope this final personal story will help you better understand the importance of faith, courage, and the ability to surrender to the messages of your soul.

YOU WANT ME TO DO *WHAT*?

*In September of last year, I was enjoying my evening medita-
tion after a busy day at work. Only the candle on my altar flick-
ered through my dark living room. Deep in meditation I was
"shown" a map of the United States, and on that map there was
a highlight around a particular state in the Pacific Northwest I'd
never visited. As a matter of fact, I had never been to any part of
the Pacific Northwest. I asked silently in meditation what was
the purpose of the highlighted map. I was told in the manner that
information is given me, that I was being asked to move to that
state. Not only was the message coming to me and through me to
move to that state, but when I asked for specifics, I was given the
exact name of the city.*

*When I came out of the meditation, I quietly asked out loud
how I was to make the move happen. And why was I being asked
to go there? I didn't hear an answer. My mind began to dart all
over the place questioning the validity of the message. I had been
living in Arizona for twenty years and prior to this meditation
had not even entertained the notion of moving. My mind came
up with a dozen reasons why this request wasn't logical. I had
two more years on my office lease. I had over a hundred clients
who relied on me. I loved my home, and financially it just wasn't
feasible to move. Additionally, I reminded the Universe, my doctor had just given me some terrifying news about my health. Where
would I get the strength to uproot my life? (At the time, I failed to
observe that uprooting my life might be the very thing required to
uproot what was physically ailing me.)*

*Let me backtrack here for a moment to give you a clear pic-
ture of the chain of events that led up to what was about to occur.
In April of the previous year, I had decided to sublet a part of my
office space because I had much more than I needed. With the*

*way my offices were set up, a wall could easily be erected to di-
vide the space, and both my clients' and my privacy would not be
invaded by the new tenant. Two weeks after I made that decision
and asked the landlord's permission, an engineering consultant
with a growing firm came in and fell in love with the space. As he
put it, "the energy felt great" and he knew he was meant to be
there.*

*We had a wall put up between the suites and he moved his
employees in. From the day we met, there was an easy familiar-
ity between us. We became fast friends, and he frequently came
over to my office just to get away from the hectic pace of his.
Often, over the next few months, he told me he wanted my office
space, too. He said the energy in my office was soothing to him
and afforded him a feeling of privacy that he didn't have in his
offices. My standard reply was, "Michael, I love it here, and I'm
not going anywhere."*

*So, back to the story. I went to work the next day, the mes-
sage of the meditation lingering in me. As was typical, I was at
my office until 8 p.m., and so was Michael who also tended to
work long hours. As I was leaving for the night, we walked out of
our respective doors at the same time. For the twentieth time, he
said, "You know I want your office space. Please let me have it."*

*I began to respond as usual, but before I could finish, he said,
"Come on, Maureen, everybody has their price. I'll pay you to
move into another space. I need your offices so I can get away
from everybody else for my sanity!"*

*This was a sign and I knew it, but I was afraid. The answers
to my questions about how my move would be possible were coming much too fast for me. I laughed and named a ridiculous sum
of money as my price for moving. He said, "I'll consider it."*

*I was amazed that he didn't dismiss it immediately. The next
day I called my attorney to see if this arrangement would even
be legal. He laughed and said, "Maureen, why would a smart*

businessman pay you that much money, and pay the rent for the space on top of that?" I asked him to please just answer the question. He replied that yes, it was legal, and then added, "It will never happen."

Several days went by and I was relieved that I hadn't heard anything more from Michael. If I had, then what would I do? I wasn't in the mood to change my life that drastically, although I was well aware that if I didn't pay attention to my physical health, my life would be changed drastically for me. Two weeks later, Michael strolled into my office one evening and said, "I'll give you half of what you asked for."

Stunned, because it was still a lot of money, I quickly said yes. I knew without question that my soul was asking me to surrender the office I loved so much and that this was Step One for the way to be made clear for me. This was the first of many surrenders on this particular journey. We shook hands on the deal and he gave me six weeks to vacate.

I went home, shaking and in a state of shock. What had I just agreed to? I'd made a commitment and there was no turning back. I sat down on the sofa and took some deep breaths. Then I meditated to still myself. In my stillness, what I could comprehend at this point, was that I was being given an opportunity to heal my physical body without distraction and financial concern. The map was "shown" to me again and I "heard" that I was to keep moving forward. The next day I began to make arrangements to wrap up my business. Six weeks later I moved out of my office.

For the next two months, I listened to my life, had a necessary surgery, and tended to my health. I made plans more than once to visit the state where I was being guided to move but, each time, my physical body wasn't up to the trip. I rested, went through a process of intense detoxification, changed my diet, journaled, meditated, and continued to listen to my life. Three days before *the new year, I clearly received a soul message to put my house up for sale.*

"Dear God," I implored, "I haven't even seen this place you want me to move to." That comment apparently held no weight, and I was guided to sell my house anyway. I put it on the market. I had surrendered my entire life, to see where the road would lead me. At that particular juncture in my life, I was more afraid of not listening to the messages coming from within than of doing things that had people speculating as to my sanity. I had had enough experience with the limited perspective of my mind interfering with the infinite possibilities offered by the Universe.

Now I was feeling a bit gutsy, or maybe I was still scared and subconsciously looking to buy more time, so I listed my house for $10,000 more than my next-door neighbors had gotten for their house two weeks prior. My house sold eight weeks later for $1,000 more than my asking price. The buyer loved it and claimed that she wanted to ensure her position since there was another offer on its way to my realtor. I surrendered my house. I had seven weeks to move out and presumably head for this new state I had still never seen. I decided to rent an apartment where I was in Arizona until I could find a place to live at my new destination.

I put three-quarters of my belongings in storage and, with my cat Sidney and the last quarter of my stuff, moved into an apartment. Both Sidney and I became very depressed. What in the world was I doing with my life or, better yet, what was being done to my life? As in the dark as I felt, I was committed to following the dots.

Ten days later, a friend came to stay with Sidney at my apartment, and I went to the Pacific Northwest at last, to the small city to which I had been guided. My plan was to find a place to live. I had decided it would be best to rent for a year before I made a purchase. My desires and expectations in a place to live were the same whether I bought or leased a home, and I put these specifics out to the Universe. *Where I live and how I live is sacred to me,* I reminded the ocean of Life.

Big-city girl meets small-city life. Oh, my God! I arrived on a little plane at a little airport in a little city where I knew no one. I wasn't coming for vacation, to do a television appearance, to give a seminar, or visit a friend. I was coming to live. I stayed at a bed and breakfast that had been recommended to me.

My goal over the next five days was to find a house, not an apartment. I met with every property manager in the city. I looked at twenty houses and felt miserable in every one of them. The weather was horrible and, for four nights running, I returned to the bed and breakfast in tears. I am certain that the owner was in fear of me having a complete breakdown, so she befriended me. She took me out for dinner, made me great breakfasts that were in harmony with my nutritional needs, and baked chocolate chip cookies and put them in my room for comfort (though I couldn't eat them, the gesture warmed my heart). She invited me to a play (I declined because my misery was wearing me out) and even went with me one day to look at houses.

I kept asking God to show me something that would give me a clue as to what I was doing here. This is what I got. Next to the bed was a copy of TV Guide. I looked in the back of it and read my horoscope for the week: "You would be wise not to oppose a change this week, no matter how great your initial resistance. With Pluto, planet of transformation, dominant, your best course of action is to go with the flow. What you stand to gain is greater than anything you might lose." I ripped out the horoscope and used it thereafter as a life raft, reading it whenever I began to question what I was doing. I knew enough to trust the message…and the Messenger (there are no coincidences). I knew that God did not bring me this far to leave me by myself.

I left on the fifth day, not liking one thing about the little city. I left with no house, no prospects, and no clarity. Now I was really confused. Had I somehow misinterpreted the message? Maybe I had interpreted the map incorrectly and I was in the wrong state. Who knew? The owner of the bed and breakfast drove me to the airport. She asked me what I was going to do. "I guess I'll come back in a few weeks and look again," I answered. On the plane, I "heard" a Voice say, "Go home and have the knee surgery that you have put off for months."

"Knee surgery!" I exclaimed. "I don't want to go through any more surgeries, any more misery, or anything else." For several months, I'd been aware that I had a torn meniscus in my knee, and I was putting off having the surgery because it seemed that I had a few more important things to do. When the tear was originally diagnosed, the doctor told me it was a simple surgery and I would only be on crutches for a day or two.

I came home and followed the guidance. Two weeks later, I was in surgery. When I woke up, the doctor informed me that the surgery was much more extensive than anticipated. He told me that I would be on crutches for four to six weeks, and that I had to go to physical therapy three days a week and use a machine at home that would move my leg 1,500 times a day. This wasn't what I'd signed on for!

I was unable to do one thing for myself, including bending down to feed my cat, so my best friend stayed with me for a week after the surgery. She waited on me hand and foot. I apologized fifty times a day for inconveniencing her, and burst into tears as spontaneously as one would burst into song. Feeling like an invalid, I was outraged that I couldn't even carry a cup of water from one room to another without help. I had never depended on anybody like this before. This was an extremely uncomfortable feeling for me and my despair was sinking even deeper, if that was possible. When she suggested I find the humor in all of this, had I had a knife in my hand I wouldn't have been responsible for my actions. When she suggested that perhaps it was time to let others help me in my life, that got my attention.

My new friend from the bed and breakfast called and I informed her of my dilemma. She announced that she was going to look for a place for me to live. She said that she felt she had a pretty good feel for what I wanted, and she would find it. Just as I started to protest, I was reminded of "letting other people help me." This, however, was a bit much. You would have thought this woman had other things to do besides look for a place for me to live, which was no easy task. Her generosity of Spirit was incredible, considering she had only known me for four days. This was something that only a lifelong friend would attempt, and even that would be unexpected. People tell me that it is hard to buy me Christmas presents. Imagine someone I just met finding a home for me in another state. Better yet, imagine me letting them! I surrendered looking for a house for myself (what choice did I have in the moment?) and gave it over to a virtual stranger. This must be some kind of cosmic joke, I told myself. "Have at it," I said to the Universe.

At some point during the third week on crutches, my life and all of its happenings actually began to amuse me. I must have lost my mind somewhere between leaving my office and selling my house. (It's a good thing I did, or I would have been in deep waters with my mind leading this parade.) I continued to go to physical therapy, became enamored in appreciation of my leg and what it does for me, and spurred on everybody else in physical therapy. I continued to write The Nature of Bliss (up until this chapter), sat back with a bowl of popcorn, and waited to see what would happen next in my life.

Framed on my bedroom wall was a saying: "My life is like a movie in which I get to play myself and I get to experience it one frame at a time. It is a foregone conclusion that the film has a happy ending—it's in the script. I love this film. I love my part and, if I play my cards right, there's a good chance I'll get an Academy Award!" I decided to continue to stay out of the way of my life.

Three weeks later, just as I got off the crutches (I find their part in my life so interesting—something I had to depend on), my bed and breakfast friend called. She announced she had found the perfect house, but I had to act quickly since this place, she said, would be snatched up in a matter of days. She followed that with, "Maureen, this house is so you." How could she be so sure? I asked myself—she doesn't know me. Now I had another dilemma, which required another leap of faith. I wasn't physically able to get there to see the house that quickly. Although I was no longer using crutches, I was limping and unable to put weight on my leg for a significant amount of time. I meditated, prayed, and was guided to trust what was occurring and to secure the house. More faith.

I called the owner of the home, asked her several questions, took a deep breath, and sent her a large deposit. I gave my thirty-day notice to the management company of the apartment where I was living, sat down with my very distressed cat, and asked him to forgive me for turning his comfortable life inside out. I started to pack again, prayed for the restoration of my strength and health, and asked God and all of my angels and guides to surround Sidney and me with their love and light as we made our way to the Pacific Northwest.

There is a reason that I am going to digress again for a moment. I would like to give you a glimpse of the machinations of the mind and how wrong it can be in spite of the fact that we are so sure about what we think we know to be true based on our past experiences.

I treat my cat, Sidney, the way I would treat a beloved child. His happiness and well-being are of great importance to me. Sidney has never been particularly adaptable. Part of my concern in making this out-of-state move was how Sidney would be able to handle the journey, as well as another new home and a very different climate. When I sold our home and we moved into the apartment, he either stayed under the bed or in the closet for the majority of the day. He had never done anything like this in his life. His seclusion lasted for over three months. Whereas for eleven years, he'd slept curled up next to me and welcomed me with kisses the second my eyes opened, he was now having no part of me. My once playful and loving cat was as withdrawn and angry with me as any person I had ever met.

I took Sidney to the veterinarian, which was never an enjoyable event. Sidney would carry on from the moment we got into the car until the moment we got back home, yowling and thrashing around. He would act as though I were taking him to an execution. I told the vet that Sidney needed an antidepressant immediately and would certainly need tranquilizers to get through our move. We talked at length about the best possible way to transport Sidney. My vet shook his head, looked at me sympathetically (he knew Sidney very well after eleven years), and said, "Maureen, whichever way you choose—car or airplane—is not going to be pleasant for either one of you." He also said, "I don't want to prescribe any kind of sedative for him because cats have a tendency to become more hyperactive when the drug wears off."

Sidney and I went back to the apartment. He went directly to his hideout under the bed and I felt like going into the closet. Instead, I prayed and asked God to please tell me which would be the best way for this move to happen for the highest good of Sidney. I was willing to do anything (although it is a well-known fact that I will only drive in a car for a maximum of three hours). The message came back to me that I was to drive to our new home. I surrendered my resistance to driving not just for a few hours, but for twenty hours.

One of my friends suggested that it would help to give Sidney two different types of homeopathic remedies throughout the trip. She said if he wouldn't take the liquid in his mouth, then I should put it on the tips of his ears. I bought enough for both of us. I worked myself up into quite a dramatic state, "knowing for sure" that Sidney would have the worst experience of his life, probably hate our new home, and most likely die still hiding under a bed. Since I felt "so sure" of it, I almost decided against listening to the message of my soul that guided me to move. But not listening, I knew, was not an option. I had to trust that Sidney would be protected. I prayed until the second we got in the car to start our trip.

We journeyed the twenty hours to the Pacific Northwest. Sidney didn't make a sound. This was so incredible to me that I kept putting my hand on him to see if he was breathing. He would look at me with his huge green eyes and I became aware that he trusted me. He stayed curled up in his very cozy carrier with his ears damp from homeopathic remedies (my ears were dripping from the remedies). We spent one night in a hotel, where he tried to get under the bed but couldn't, and the next day, we got back into the car and drove the last ten hours. He never made a sound.

I stopped for gas one last time. We were fifteen minutes from the new home we'd never seen. I read the directions that the owner of the house had sent me and realized I was holding my breath. I took several deep breaths and tears flooded my eyes. I'd done it. I'd really done it. I looked at Sidney and thanked him for being amazing. I stayed with that awareness for several minutes. I knew in that moment that everything was going to be fine.

We drove up to our new home. As I walked inside, a breeze wafted ever so gently over me. I knew angels surrounded me and I felt the presence of my father who had journeyed to the other side twenty-three years before. I felt the house embrace us with love. I felt as though it had been waiting for me for a long time. I unzipped Sidney's carrier and we explored the house together. It took him no time to find all of his now-favorite sun spots. He was enamored with all the birds and squirrels and, later, deer (all of which he continues to watch in quiet reverence). I was enamored with how the Universe works. We were home and we both knew it.

I went into the backyard, lifted my arms to the heavens, and simply said, "Thank you God for blessing me." Later I was reminded to thank myself for having the faith and the courage to surrender to wisdom far greater than my own. I also showered thanks upon my angel friend from the bed and breakfast.

Over the next four weeks, I finished writing this book, in a state of bliss. Life had returned to both Sidney and me with great joy, grace, and peace. Later it became clear to me that I had been asked to move to this new place because here there is a quietness in people's souls and a peace in their footsteps. Here, community is more important than opportunity. Here, connection to each other and all that is Life is much more important than the rush of modern-day life. This influence has supported my lifelong quest for peace and Oneness.

COMING HOME TO BLISS

How we experience our life depends on how willing we are to listen to our soul and how willing we are to travel with an often heavy load. My story is but one of millions of stories of people who have suffered loss and hardship and risen to something more magnificent, grand, and beautiful than what was shattered. I used my story simply because I know its every detail.

Spiritual journeys often begin with a fall. The question is: Will you let the fall define you? How will you get up from the fall and reclaim your life? Will your ego's resistance and insistence be the bane of your existence? Will you fall apart in a million shards and stay broken, or will you put yourself back together again? Are you willing to steady yourself after a fall, find the blessing, retrieve the message, and venture forward?

In *The Divine Comedy*, Dante wrote: "Oh human race! Born to ascend on wings, why do ye fall at such a little wind?"

Remember that the Breath of God blesses you. The message of the soul guides you. Much time is wasted working and struggling (by virtue of the limited perspective of the mind) through the tensions and emotions of life. The message of *The Nature of Bliss* is to come back to your authentic nature, go beyond your tensions and illusions, and remember to flow through life with love. When you are in the flow, you will experience your extraordinary self and feel both significant to and wonderfully humble before all of creation. You can call forth creative energy and see it manifest as it shows you your immeasurable talent. When you are in the flow, you become more beautiful and radiant and glorious than at any other time or age in your life; you are healed of the maladies of the body, mind, and spirit.

When you are in the flow, you will know for yourself that the veils are lifted and there is no separation between you and God.

You now hold in your hands the map. Do with it as you will. The attainment of bliss is yours to achieve on your own. Listen to your soul's message to guide your life. Open your heart and live well. Search for the revelation of Who You Are. God bless you.

Namaste.